Is Your Digital Front Door Unlocked?

Your Key to Privacy and Security in the Digital Age

Gary Davis

DEDICATION

For my children, Sean and Amber.

You've given me a lifetime of love and laughter and all sorts of inspiration for this book.

CONTENTS

ACKNOWLEDGMENTS

I have been blessed with a lifetime of relationships and experiences from guiding hands and attentive ears to inspire and shape this book. I often muse that my journey isn't one I could have easily mapped. Instead, I've followed a path of sensing the things I have a passion for and allowing myself to embrace those passions. Such a path can work if you surround yourself with people you can trust to have your best interests at heart. With that in mind, I've had the pleasure of befriending and working with world-class individuals who were instrumental in crafting this book.

I extend my sincerest appreciation to my writing partner, Pete Gade, and to editor Mary Keils. Pete's tireless efforts in shaping and guiding revisions helped transform an idea for a book into a compelling story arc with a conversational tone that stitches the notion of our digital journey into an engaging and enjoyable read. Mary brought a welcome extra set of eyes for spotting needed fixes and applying the polish. Trust me when I say that writing a book is much harder than most think it is, and it was an absolute pleasure working with Pete and Mary to bring this book to life.

I would also like to express my gratitude to the companies I worked for while contemplating how best to structure this book. For the past ten years both McAfee and Intel gave me the freedom to pursue this book while being rich sources of research and subject matter to draw from. Specifically, I would like to thank the following McAfee colleagues: Judith Bitterli for that gentle nudge to put pen to paper, or rather hand to keyboard; John Giamatteo for trusting me to be the voice of McAfee's Consumer business; Chris Young for hearing me out on the importance of getting this book published; Raj Samani and the Advanced Threat Research (ATR) team for bouncing ideas around with me; and, parenting sage Toni Birdsong for providing deep insights around parenting in a digital world. I would also like to thank my PR and Social Media partners Jaime Le, Ashley Dolezal, and Sarah Grayson for their assistance in creating a solid marketing and promotion plan. Karen Azevedo did an absolutely incredible job laying out a world-class cover for which I am grateful. I could go on and on as I think about all those who gave me ideas, inspiration, and support. Suffice it to say that I have many to be thankful to.

As you can imagine, writing a book is a labor of love that disrupts the normal course of any life. I would like to thank my guiding light, Carla Pascoaleto, for allowing us to forgo a social life for several months so I could hunker down nights and weekends to work on the book. And let's not forget about my faithful companions, Lunna and Laura, our German Shepherds, who flanked me in my office and offered an occasional welcome respite from the rigors of writing a book to throw them balls.

I would also like to express my sincerest appreciation to my children Sean and Amber (and their spouses Rachel and Mike) for giving me years of directly applicable hands-on experience and agreeing to reference those experiences in the book. And none of this would have been possible if it weren't for the love and support from my mom and my siblings—especially my older brother Greg, who likely has the strongest aversion to technology of anyone I know. Writing a book about online security and privacy that Greg would enjoy set the bar high.

I would also like to thank my good friend Bruce Snell, who has always been there to ideate around security and privacy topics. And finally, I would like to thank Hacking Exposed co-authors Stuart McClure and George Kurtz, who recruited me to work at McAfee and set me on the journey to ultimately write this book.

INTRODUCTION

Just in case you have any doubts, this book is for you.

Whether you're a mom, dad, daughter, son, sister, brother, aunt, uncle, grandma, grandpa, or godparent, you probably use the internet. Maybe a little. Maybe a lot. Either way, you're on it. In fact, you've left your mark all over the internet—and to a much greater degree than you're aware of.

It's amazing how much we rely on the internet and yet how little we know about it. Certainly, we have a strong sense of the ways it helps us in our daily lives: We get our news on it. We chat with friends on it. We set our home alarm, access our grades, and even plot our quickest route home on it. Not to mention how we shop, bank, book vacations, and look up questions about our health on it. And it's safe to say that an understanding of the internet ends there for most folks. But that's certainly not the case if we switch things around. The frank truth: We know very little about the internet, but the internet knows a lot about us—an awful lot. Some would argue that it knows many things about us that even our loved ones don't.

This book pulls back the curtains on the internet and shows how eagerly it slurps up the personal information you create when you hop on social media, use mapping apps, connect that new thing in your home, or do practically anything else online. It'll also show you the impact internet use has on your security and privacy in a world where other parties have a big incentive to capture, analyze, and capitalize upon your data—whether they are legitimate businesses or cybercrooks or creeps.

This book isn't out to scare you. It's here to motivate you and empower you to confidently enjoy your time online. My aim is to put you in control of your security and privacy, your family's too, with an even-handed look at the most prevalent challenges facing individuals and families today. It skips the scare tactics that can dominate the topic and illustrates the steps each of us can take to lead more secure and private lives in an increasingly connected world.

Because this book is for people in families of any size or structure, the book looks at security and privacy across the stages of a family's life and the roles each of us play in those stages (from birth to the time we eventually leave a digital legacy behind), along with important milestones and transitional periods in between. You'll see how security and privacy are pertinent at every step of your digital journey and how specific age groups have concerns that are often unique to that stage of life. It's also important to note that although I address the security and privacy activities typically found in a given life stage, your mileage will vary. There are no hard rules as to when on your digital journey you may experience something that needs tending to.

No matter where you find yourself on your digital journey right now, my hope is that you'll read this book cover to cover. Doing so will change your understanding and use of the internet. Moreover, I hope you'll keep this book handy as a reference. Nothing would make me happier than to see it in your hands at your favorite coffee shop and notice lots of Post-it notes, dog-eared pages, and highlighted sections. The table of contents has all the pressing topics and issues called out, ready for you to lean on when you need them.

Ultimately this book, like most things in life, is about choice. You can choose to roll the dice and hope you're not either one of the hundreds of millions who are victims each year of phishing scams, ransomware attacks, and identity theft or among the handful of those who still fall for the Nigerian prince lottery scam. Or you can choose to embrace the guidelines outlined herein and make it orders of magnitude more difficult for a bad actor or cybercriminal to make a victim of you or your loved ones. That you have picked up this book tells me you're well on your way to a safer, more private digital destiny and more enjoyable online experiences overall.

So, no matter how you choose to start, I'm simply glad that you're starting. Every journey starts with an all-important first step. The singular aim of this book is to make the internet a safer and more pleasant place for you and your family—and you'll see you have plenty of power to make that happen. Let's get to it …

Gary Davis

1

IT ALL STARTS WITH YOUR DATA LAKE

You may not know this, but you're the proud owner of a lake.

This is no ordinary lake. You can't see it, even though it gets larger every day. There are no cool breezes rolling off it, nor will you spot any paddleboarders gliding along on it or see quaint A-frame vacation homes lining its shores. In fact, this lake is not even filled with water. It's filled with data, and plenty of it. Data about you.

More specifically, you own a "data lake." It's a term that technologists typically use, but for us, using the term *data lake* paints a strong visual for an important concept—you create a lot of data about yourself simply by going online and using connected devices. Your interactions online create drops of data that collect into streams that pool together to form an ever-deepening lake of more and more data over time. That's how you became the owner of your data lake; and it's rippling with all kinds of personal information so vast and specific that it's a near-perfect mirror reflection of you.

This notion of a data lake isn't new. For decades we've had plenty of personal data attached to us, like our medical records, Social Security numbers, tax returns, date of birth, credit history, and so on. What *is* new, relatively speaking, is the internet. More exactly, what's new is the way the internet is used as a tool to collect, store, and use all this data.

Once, not long ago, data was nestled in paper files or stored on isolated computer networks housed in glassed-off air-conditioned rooms. Now, data is digital, moves effortlessly, and gets accessed from devices and places around the world at breakneck speeds. This makes it possible for businesses, organizations, and even individuals to collect and analyze such data for a whole host of purposes— advertising, creating insurance proposals, scientific research, to name but a few. This also creates entirely new opportunities for cybercrime and malicious deeds; the billions of records collectively held by major retailers, credit reporting agencies, email marketing list aggregators, and other organizations present themselves as prime targets for cybercriminals and nation-state organizations. And you can imagine why those records are so attractive; they contain all manner of personal information like your name, email address, phone numbers, physical address, gender, date of birth, personal mortgage amounts, interest rates, social media accounts, and characterizations of your credit scores. In the hands of a cybercriminal, those records can be forged into personalized skeleton keys that unlock a host of follow-on crimes, like identity theft, fraud, extortion, and embezzlement. Such crimes aren't new, but some methods being used to commit them are, such as bad links seeded into search results, phishing emails designed to make you hand over your passwords, or phony tech support pop-up ads that show up while you're browsing. Think of it this way: if crime follows the money, cybercriminals have set up operations on the internet because there's plenty of money to be made in data. Personal data to be exact.

Here's what else is new with regards to our data lakes: the way we live our modern connected lives.

That's to say we've changed too since the internet came along. Aside from all the personal information we create by way of interacting with institutions such as banks, insurance companies, and federal agencies, we're creating volumes of additional personal information on the internet by simply using our computers, mobile devices, and other internet-connected things. It began on computers with cookies that tracked our browsing habits. Then the internet wove its way into smartphones and added location tracking into the mix (because we keep our phones within arm's reach nearly 24 hours a day). Now it's embedded in our cars, home alarm systems, appliances, voice-activated assistants, and the locks on our front doors, even as it tracks our behaviors across those connected devices too. For example, insurance companies will give you "good driver discounts" if you plug in a little device that shares your driving data with them. (And, just so you're aware, your insurance company's idea of good driving and yours may be altogether different.) Utility companies are installing "smart meters" that monitor your energy usage, and you might even have a connected thermostat at home to save a few bucks on your bills or perhaps connected cameras to keep an eye on the house while you're away.

Meanwhile, we've ramped up our personal use of the internet to entirely new levels as well. Stop for a moment and consider about how much data you're creating and what *kind* of data you're creating. It's all quite personal. We're talking your financial transactions, location data derived from your mobile app when you go for a run or walk, what you search for, the websites you visit, your music preferences, your purchasing habits and history—and it's also all the emails, documents, photos, and videos you create and save in the cloud or post on social media.

The thing you should realize is that you're generating and *sharing* this personal data right now. Sometimes you share it knowingly, like when you post a picture on Facebook. Other times, it happens beneath the surface without you really knowing it, such as when you generate personal data by using a voice-activated assistant that captures what you buy, search, when you set the alarm for the night, and so on. Most often, such exchanges occur contractually. Remember when you clicked yes on that company's user agreement for your latest app or online service? Buried somewhere in the legalese of that multi-page form was likely some language that allows the company to collect usage data or even personal data. What's more, the company may share this data with its partners or other companies in turn, again per your user agreement. Hear that rush of water? That's you, filling up your data lake with even more personal information, which has a dollar value of its own.

To put it bluntly, our increasing reliance on technology has us sharing far more information about ourselves than we even realize and doing so without a full understanding of the risks involved.

What's at Stake on the Internet

In a couple of words, security and privacy.

Let's start with security, as it's probably the issue you're most familiar with. As consumers, we've been messaged about internet security for some time now. We've heard how we should protect ourselves with strong passwords and that we should change them regularly; we've been cautioned not to click on sketchy links or to open emails from suspicious sources; and we've used antivirus protection on our computers to protect us from hackers—all to increase our security and make us less susceptible to cybercrime. On the corporate and institutional side of security, you can imagine the never-ending cat-and-mouse game taking place between large organizations as they look to fend off breaches and attacks by cybercriminals, not to mention similar matches of wits between different nation-states as they attempt to keep (and steal) vital information from each other. Yet the important thing to remember is that behind every cybercrime is another person or a group of people. Crimes are orchestrated and committed by people, not by machines. It's easy to lose sight of that because we're talking about networks, computers, files, and records, all of which can feel intangible, technical, or both. As we go through this book together, let's keep in mind that in matters of internet security, people are the crooks and victims—and that cybercrime exacts a human toll.

As for privacy, that topic is relatively new to the scene, and thus far less known (and understood) by the general public. Up until the rise of the commercial internet, you had a strong sense of when, where, and with whom you were sharing your information. That's changed. Consider social media. If your social media settings are set to public, do you know who has viewed that picture of you and your family on vacation? You can't say for sure. And that social media platform itself, what does a company like Facebook know about you based upon the articles you've read from your newsfeed, the brands and popular personalities you follow, and the videos you've watched or ads you've clicked on? Quite a bit. With the commercial internet, billions of exchanges take place every day where people share their information in exchange for a free service like Facebook at no out-of-pocket cost. In these so-called value exchanges, your personal data is the currency of the day. The same is true for many of the apps you use. Similarly, companies and developers offer them for free. Again, they're not truly free. Look at the user agreements for some of your apps and once again wade into the world of legalese. The language therein may tell you that the apps you're using may very well access other data on your phone, like your contacts, your photo library, your calendar, your texts, and your travels (via location services), which the developer can then transform into cash by selling to other parties in some form or other. Perhaps you have heard over this past year how effortlessly your information has flowed between organizations you've never heard of and, of course, maybe some you have. That's given rise to the popular notion of a data economy where businesses don't make money by selling their apps—they make money by selling data collected by their apps. Much of this business behavior is legal (again, read your user agreements, if you can get through them).

Some of these business behaviors aren't legitimate or are at the very least exploitative, like the spate of malicious Pokémon Go apps that shot up in 2016 during the height of the Pokémon Go craze, which suspiciously collected more information than they needed to play a simple game.[1] Note that such questionable or downright malicious apps don't make it onto people's phones by accident. They're downloaded on purpose often by those who don't know they're installing a fraudulent app. And further note that people aren't downloading them from sketchy sources on the internet. You can find malicious apps like these often in legitimate app stores, even as the app store operators attempt to keep them off their online shelves.

In all, these practices continue, yet people are waking up to them. Even legitimate instances of data collection are under fire from the public and lawmakers alike, as we'll explore later in this book.

---

[1] https://www.computerworld.com/article/3095428/a-surge-of-pokemon-go-related-apps-is-out-to-steal-your-data.html

It's true that if you use the internet, you're handing over personal information to another party to some degree or other. Whether you know it or not. Sometimes your data is "anonymized" so that it's difficult to be used to identify you outright. But sometimes it includes things like your name, address, date of birth, Social Security number, or credit card number—things that directly identify you and that are painful, if not impossible, to change if they are stolen from you. From the collection of data, others can infer your likes, dislikes, personal opinions on a topic, even your age and physical well-being—all with an eerie degree of accuracy thanks to the use of modern-day analytics and artificial intelligence. For example, later in this book I'll share the story of how a large retailer used big data about a customer's purchases and sent coupons for baby clothes and cribs to a teenager weeks before she told her father that she was pregnant. If that's not a privacy issue, I don't know what is. Welcome to our world today.

What's at Stake for You and Your Family

I honestly believe that we live in amazing days, and I hope that comes through while reading this book. Too many times you'll come across articles or stories that make it seem like the internet is out to get you. The truth is that the world of the internet is like our world of neighborhoods, cities, and countries. It has its shopping centers, financial districts, schools, movie theaters, and libraries, each of which offer a multitude of benefits. We're far better off for having the internet in our lives, yet we must recognize that like any community it also has its shady back alleys. Just as you know how to get around safely in your neighborhood, my aim is to help you get around more safely on the internet. A lot of it comes down to street smarts and good habits, and that's what I'll share through examples from my decades of working in digital security and my experiences as a son, brother, father, and friend and an everyday internet user just like you.

So, let's see what's at stake.

With regards to security, we need to realize the *tremendous* value our data and personal information holds to businesses and cybercrooks alike. For businesses, the analysis of our data and personal information can provide them with tremendous insights into our habits, behaviors, relationships, finances, travels, purchasing, and even our health. They can use these insights to market to us, sell to us, and, in some cases, assign certain risks to us. Moreover, they can sell these insights to other parties. Data brokers make millions of dollars by collecting information about consumers from public and private sources and selling it to other companies and organizations. In the case of cybercrime, a single breached record can be worth roughly ten times the value of a breached credit card.[2] This is because certain information such as Social Security numbers and dates of birth is difficult if not impossible to change. Cybercriminals and fraudsters can use records like your mother's maiden name again and again to commit multiple acts of fraud or embezzlement.

Whether it's collected legally or illegally, your data, and your family's data, is a new form of currency.[3] It has value. And others covet it. You must think of your data and personal information like the cash in your wallet and the funds in your bank. They belong to you. No one has the right to simply take it without your clear knowledge and consent.

For privacy, the stakes are understandably personal. What you share with others, businesses, and even governments should be up to you as well. That's the way the world views privacy. It's little wonder that in 2019, 181 national constitutions mention the right to privacy.[4] As a global society, we believe that what's private should stay that way. Unfortunately, today's internet isn't necessarily set up that way. We can point to rather extreme examples of where businesses have taken advantage of our trust or assumption that our interactions online are private. (Note the December 2018 *New York*

---

[2] https://www.networkworld.com/article/2880366/anthem-hack-personal-data-stolen-sells-for-10x-price-of-stolen-credit-card-numbers.html

[3] https://www.forbes.com/sites/michelleevans1/2018/03/12/why-data-is-the-most-important-currency-used-in-commerce-today/#6967e9a354eb

[4] https://www.constituteproject.org/search?lang=en&key=privacy

Times article that broke the news Facebook had allegedly given Netflix and Spotify the ability to read the private messages of users without their knowledge.[5]) We can also point to the broad use of data collection practices mentioned above, when combined with data analysis, can infer a great deal about you with alarming accuracy. (Once again, I mention the major retailer that effectively guessed a teenage girl was pregnant based on an analysis of her purchasing habits.) Sadly, we largely do not know these activities are taking place—when and where this data is being collected, by whom, with whom it's being shared, and for what purpose.

The stakes get yet more personal because some of our own behavior can put us at risk. The internet is a platform with a global reach and a forever memory. What you say, what you do, what you post can have a lifetime of implications. As a family, each member has a personal responsibility to look after themselves and each other. This unwritten contract extends to the internet because our actions there can impact our personal and professional lives, not to mention the lives of others. This book is laden with examples of how people get passed over for jobs, ruin romantic relationships, and end up doing actual physical harm to others because of what they say, do, or post online, ranging from sharing a picture of someone passed out at a party because it seemed funny at the time or something calculated and intentionally injurious like cyberbullying. Some of the most damaging things that can happen online come about by our own actions. It's not a business secretly collecting data bringing about the harm; the blame lies with us. In a time where we see articles that look to blame the internet for the loss of civility and good manners in our society, isn't it time we looked at ourselves as part of the problem—and ultimately the solution?

What Did We Learn?

It's time for us to realize and take ownership of our role in leading a more secure and private life in the digital age. We must get much smarter about how the internet works and how it manages information about us, particularly as 25% of Americans say they go

---

[5] https://www.nytimes.com/2018/12/18/technology/facebook-privacy.html

online "almost constantly" (a number that rockets up to 39% for ages 18–29[6]). You can see this for yourself by going to any street corner, mall, airport, or other place where people gather and seeing almost everyone glued to their smartphone. When we gain more knowledge about security and privacy on the internet, we can make better decisions. Additionally, we can take more personal responsibility for our behaviors because we're aware of their repercussions.

Your first step on this journey is to understand what data is being collected from you, who's collecting it, why they're collecting it, and what they're doing with it (like if they're sharing it with other companies or individuals and what security measures they're taking to protect it). I won't mince words: this is a challenge, but it can be done. That's why I've written this book. After all, there are coyotes stalking your data lake. You may not see them, not right away, but they're out there—corporations and cybercriminals in search of a cool drink of data and personal information all about you.

By taking a comprehensive look at your digital life from birth to legacy, this book shows how you can protect yourself and your family as you all make your way in a world where digital connections and lakes of data are the new normal. My hope is that this book will enable you to create a culture of security and privacy within your home that you can take forward into your workplace and community. By planting the seed, you will be a champion for creating a safer internet and online experiences for everyone.

---

[6] http://www.pewresearch.org/fact-tank/2018/03/14/about-a-quarter-of-americans-report-going-online-almost-constantly/

2

BIRTH TO AGE 2 – FIRST FOOTPRINTS

Your baby makes his or her first digital footprint the moment he or she is born. Often before.

When your baby is on the way, their privacy and digital security is probably the last thing you have on your mind. At least it's way down there on the list—of course it is! What else could be on your mind? Oh, about a million things. You're preparing for a bright, joyous addition to your family and home. Everything you're doing is intended to create an environment that is safe and comfortable, so your baby knows a warm and loving world right from the start. Not to mention, you and your family are anticipating how much you'll enjoy these moments too.

Part of that enjoyment is the sharing, which in most cases today means online. (When's the last time you took a picture on film and had it printed?) From digital invitations to baby showers hosted at home to ultrasound pictures posted on social media, the weeks and months leading up to birth are a celebration as well. And that's where those first tiny dribbles into baby's data lake begin. Your first posts on social media qualify as their first little digital footprints, along with anything else you share about them online.

Privacy for Parents, and Baby Too

Enter *Sharenting*—a clever term thrown around nowadays to describe how parents share pictures and stories of their children online. (Sometimes to a fault.) My view on the subject is probably quite close to yours: Nothing brings me more joy than seeing my grandchildren doing cute things via my children's social media accounts. It always leaves me craving more. Wanting to share pictures of your children with your friends and family is absolutely natural. It's a celebration of parenthood and a record of your child's milestones in life. But before snapping and sharing pictures of our kiddos, parents in this digital age need to consider three points that mostly revolve around privacy:

1)   Nothing you share online is *ever* 100% private.

Even if you have your social media privacy settings locked down so that only your family and friends can see your posts, there are ways around those protections. For example, a friend could be viewing a picture, grab a screenshot of it, and share it with someone else who is not a friend of yours on social media. Another popular way of sharing locked down pictures and other content is by simply using the camera on your phone to take a picture of what's being displayed. So, just assume that whatever you share has the potential of going well beyond even the narrowest privacy settings you establish.

2)   Everything you post is permanent.

Even when you take it down from your social media account, that doesn't mean it's gone. It may live on within the social media platform's data records, or other people may have downloaded that picture to their phone or computer.

3)   Babies have a right to privacy too.

You'll always be their parent, but you won't always be in charge of them. As much as we hate to admit it, our kids grow up. And as they do, will they want to find out that some of these not-so-flattering pictures are public?

For instance, have you ever cringed at something on social media that didn't seem like the kind of thing you need (or want) to see posted about someone else's kid? Like maybe a toddler having a tantrum while a relative is laughing off to the side of the shot? Or maybe a snapshot of a potty-training moment? Think of how embarrassing that would be for you.

Now realize that it's orders of magnitude more embarrassing for that little kid, and yet more embarrassing should that video or photo suddenly appear "out of nowhere" online during their junior year of high school. Let's not forget that cyberbullying is a thing as well. You wouldn't want to see some of those pictures, cute as they are in the moment, turned against them later when they're school-age kids. (Sad to say, it happens, and we'll talk about cyberbullying in detail later in the book.) Sure, those are extreme examples, but you can sum up all these points this way: Those pictures and stories are *theirs*, not yours. It's their legacy. Until they become old enough to be the stewards of their own privacy and identity online, it's up to you to fulfill that role and to protect them—from embarrassment and intrusion.

So, as you have that camera poised, take the shot and then pause. Ask a few questions before you post. Why are you posting this? Is there any chance it could embarrass your child one day? Is there anyone in the world who shouldn't see this about your child—now or ever? Are there details in the picture that could be used to identify personal bits of information, such as a street address? It's common today for college boards, employers, and even future partners to conduct social media searches about applicants, job seekers, and possible romantic interests as a sort of "digital background check." The point being that, and you'll hear this quite often throughout the book, the internet is a forever thing. What you post will end up in your baby's digital lake as part of their permanent record.

Another important part of this conversation is to make sure that you and your partner are on the same page about what's "shareworthy" and what's not. And as your baby becomes a kid who can express their preferences, you should start asking them if a particular picture, clip, or story is OK to share. As their parent and protector, it's part of your job to care for their emotional well-being. Posting embarrassing pics, or even seemingly innocent pics that they simply don't want you to post for any reason, is a big no-no as it can damage their self-esteem and their trust in you. It's a pretty big deal.

Kids are more tuned into this than we may think. They're affected by how you use social media, especially when it involves them. A study conducted by the UK Children's Commissioner's Office that centered on social media use of kids ages 8 to 12 summarized its findings as follows:

Many children spoke about how their parents would post pictures and videos of them on their own social media accounts. Children talked about feeling uncomfortable and bothered when their parents shared some photos. For some children, this was because they did not want a big group of people to see them, or did not like the way they looked, while others simply did not like being pestered and pressured by parents to share photos when they didn't want to.[7]

Granted, we've just rocketed ahead from birth announcements and baby pictures all the way up to middle school and beyond, yet here we are. That's parenting, where part of our unwritten job description is to look ahead, sometimes way ahead, to make sure we're doing right by our children as we usher them through life. Thanks to the internet, we can now add keeping them safe online and protecting their privacy to our list of things we must take on from the very start.

I get it. With everything being so social, nothing can seem more important than getting pictures and stories out to the world that capture just how adorable your new addition is. And we have the potential like never before to be inclined to rocket children to stardom, in some cases capitalizing upon their cuteness for financial gain. Increasingly, children under two are gaining millions of followers on social media. Most parents who do this will say it's from necessity due to income challenges. It can be very lucrative for those children who can capture our hearts and minds in social media, as this snippet from a *Fast Company* article on young internet stars shows:

---

[7] https://www.childrenscommissioner.gov.uk/wp-content/uploads/2018/01/Childrens-Commissioner-for-England-Life-in-Likes.pdf

There's also big money to be had on Instagram. A kid influencer can command about $100 per 1,000 followers per post, according to Kyle Helpmeet, the founder of the influencer management company God and Beauty. A child with 500,000 followers would earn about $5,000 for a single image. It only goes up from there, especially if a brand buys a campaign, which could include multiple posts, Instagram Story updates, and even an event appearance. Some influencers ask for even more per post.[8]

I struggle with that a bit, but everyone is entitled to parent the way they feel is best for them and their family. The point I want to illustrate is that you can't possibly know how this will affect your child's mental and physical well-being later in life. There are also hazards that exist in the moment:

But there are larger concerns for these Instagram parents. The internet has a dark side, one teeming with racists, sexists, pedophiles, and trolls. Nguyen-Miyoshi, mother of six-year-old Zooey, has personal experience dealing with trolls online. She worked in social media for 10 years, and during that time she posted a picture of two men who'd refused to give up their seats to pregnant women on Twitter. The post went viral, and Nguyen-Miyoshi had so many trolls come after her that she left the internet for a time.[9]

Let's roll our conversation back to where we started, to the days of infancy and toddlerhood, so we can see what else we can do to protect younger children's privacy. There are plenty of topics we can talk about, and we'll break them up into bite-sized ways you can keep them safe here and now.

Security Around the Home

If you already have a toddler on the scene, you know all about this—making umpteen little changes around the home to keep you and the kids physically safe. I remember when our children started walking or scooting around in those little buggy things, and we saw our home with entirely new eyes. There were all kinds of things they could get into and stairs they could go down. We looked around and

---

[8] https://www.fastcompany.com/90278778/the-2-year-old-instagram-influencers-who-make-more-than-you-do

[9] Ibid.

saw electric sockets waiting to be poked at with a butter knife (this happened with my son and it scared me to no end); kitchen cabinets full of family china or pots and pans that a tot could swing open with ease; and a VCR with a perfectly sized slot for sliding in half a grilled cheese sandwich. (A VCR? Yep, that was back in the day.) These things presented physical hazards, so we had to secure them. We got plastic plugs for the sockets, an interior latch for the kitchen cabinets, and a clever little plastic dam that fit into the VCR. Over time, as they got older and more mobile, we secured more and more things that were in reach.

At one point my daughter got her hands on a pair of scissors and proceeded to cut her own hair. Of course, this was before the internet and social media so we could only share her fancy haircut via a photograph with close family and friends. At one point, I even nicknamed her Thumper because of all the times I heard her come rolling down the stairs even with gates installed. In all, it was like fighting against a rising flood until, one day, they were old enough that we didn't have to worry about these things.

Why did we go through all that trouble? Actually, we didn't see it as trouble. We saw it as keeping the family safe. (Not to mention keeping our sanity.) It's a bit different and trickier for parents who need to go through and secure today's digital household. While you can quickly scan a room and see the furniture and things that need to get baby-proofed, digital security is something you can't see and requires plenty of things to tackle to keep our kids and families safe.

Baby Monitors and Other Internet-Connected Devices

What a comfort these devices are, especially with the advances in them over the years. We have video where we can check in on our sleepy-time angels and speakers so we can coo back at them. They work on our home internet networks, which means they are ultimately connected to the internet at large as well. Without proper password protection, these devices can give a motivated hacker eyes, ears, and even a voice into your home. I'm not out to scare you when I say this: it can and does happen more often than you might think.

One such story comes by way of an article from National Public Radio (NPR) here in the U.S. One mother shared a story that began with her waking up one morning to find the baby video monitor pointed right at her. It'd moved since she went to sleep, yet she assumed that her husband had been checking in on her and their baby while he was at work by way of the app used to control the camera. Turns out, a hacker was able to access their monitor even though they had assigned a unique password to it. Once they came to this realization, they unplugged the monitor and contacted the police. The hacker had clearly exploited a vulnerability in the device. Can you imagine how she and her family felt? It's heartbreaking, and this mother was blown away that this is an issue that, by her impression, people simply aren't aware of: "I would have never, ever bought something if I thought it was this easy of a security risk," she told NPR. "When I was making my baby registry, nobody warned me—no other mom said anything. It's not common knowledge."[10]

As with so many hacker scenarios, we're left to wonder why on earth would anyone do such a thing? More often than not, hackers are out for financial gain, although there are cases where it's a Peeping Tom trying to get a peek at something they shouldn't. The way it works is this: the baby monitor isn't the prize in and of itself, it's the home network and the computers and information stored on them. Your home network is only as strong as its weakest link.

You may have antivirus and good security software on your Mac or PC or smartphone, but other connected devices, like baby monitors, typically do not have security built into them at all. For example, many of these devices come with generic or default factory usernames and passwords that are common knowledge, thus making them an easy hack and an easy entry point into your home network. This is a common problem as more and more historically "dumb" devices become "smart" and connect to the internet. Some manufacturers of these devices have long made what they make and have little or no experience in digital security, so the devices aren't as thoroughly engineered for security as they should be. In fact, a

---

[10] https://www.npr.org/sections/thetwo-way/2018/06/05/617196788/s-c-mom-says-baby-monitor-was-hacked-experts-say-many-devices-are-vulnerable

couple of years HP released research showing that the top 10 devices deployed in homes had, on average, 25 vulnerabilities each.

So, what can you do?

- When you buy a connected device, change the default username and password. Use the same best practices for password creation (reference) that you would on your computer or home network. Go through and audit your existing devices too. If you find factory passwords or weak passwords in play, change them too. This is healthy practice to do on a regular basis.

- Research your baby monitor (and other devices) for security and privacy. Read reviews, search for online lists of reputable manufacturers that are baking good security and privacy into their connected products. In the case of your baby monitor, it's a window into your world, so this only makes good sense. There are several companies that when notified that they have a vulnerable device in the market will take immediate steps to fix it whereas others wait months, and in some cases years, to incorporate a fix.

- If you're not comfortable with the risks or at all unsure about the security in your device, get rid of it. Thankfully, you can still go old school with a baby monitor that doesn't connect to the internet.

- Make sure your home Wi-Fi router has a strong username and password. I've seen that many internet providers walk people through this process when they first install a Wi-Fi router in your home. In any event, now is a good time to verify that and make any changes if you find your username and password lacking.

- Look into the new breed of home network security devices that protect your home at the source—your Wi-Fi router. They provide automatic protection for your entire home network, including all connected devices without a display (like a baby monitor) and those with a display such as your smartphones and PCs. This is one of the best ways to address the issue I brought up a moment ago, where some, if not most, devices simply don't have the proper degree of security baked into them already.

The last thing I want to do is scare you with stalky stories of creeps peeping into your home, but this happens way more often than you think. However, I do want you to be aware of the risks associated with *any* connected device you bring into your home and how you can protect yourself. Bottom line: don't assume a connected device has the security you need built into it. Take the extra steps listed above to make sure it does.

Playing Your Digital Life Closer to the Vest

Baby changes everything. Your schedule. Your finances. Your sleep. And your entire outlook on life. (Did I mention sleep?) Naturally, it's easy to see these changes get reflected in your digital life as well.

A couple of pages back, we chatted about sharenting and sharing baby's life online, part of which may include baby's date of birth, baby's name, and maybe baby's nickname too. These attributes tend to show up elsewhere—like our passwords. Such names and dates will enter your mind when you come up with that next round of PINs or passwords you're asked for. Let's face it, it's much easier to remember something like your child's birthday than a completely random number. Avoid the temptation. A certain amount of hacking isn't technical at all. It's psychological and behavioral. Hackers will rely on the fact that many people will use things like birthdates and nicknames for the basis of their usernames and passwords, which gives them a jumpstart on breaking into your accounts and stealing your information or using that information in social engineering attacks. Now, I'm not saying don't share birthdays and the like. Not necessarily. Rather, just skip those things when it comes time to gin up your passwords. You can go a long way toward duping a cybercriminal with something as simple as using a birthday in reverse order, especially if you pair it with other letters and characters. The main point is do not make it easy for a bad actor to work their way into your life or home.

What I will caution you about is sharing too many aspects of your new routine. As you know, with baby comes a schedule filled with regular playdates, time at daycare, parenting groups, and even doctor visits. If you were to plot out those comings and goings, some real patterns would likely pop up. As with many moments, we can get tempted to share pictures of baby and friends visiting the same park at the same time every week. Again, we like to celebrate times like that.

However, playing your digital life closer to the vest means being mindful that sharing such enjoyable moments (like a photo of you at daycare pickup, which telegraphs where baby is during the day and when you're probably not home) risks putting your schedule in the hands of a bad actor who could use it against you—such as plotting a break-in around that information. Once more, this is an example of what's possible rather than what's common, but enjoying a routine event is not a good reason to put that information out there. The world doesn't need to know those things.

One more thing about photos: there's another way they tell a whole lot about you—through metadata. Metadata is "data about data," and in this case you can think of it as information that rides piggyback on the photos you take. Using GPS, phone cameras (and some regular cameras) can embed location information in photos, along with other info like the time, the date, the name of the device and so on. Why is there metadata for photos? Many reasons. Professional photographers use it to help ensure their work isn't stolen or claimed by someone else. There are business applications, like storing and categorizing thousands of images in databases. And so on. Now, do you need all that metadata packed into your photos? Probably not, as metadata can reveal all kinds of things, like where you live, where you play, where your favorite family restaurant is, and so on. OK, that sounds a little creepy again. Yet metadata is plenty easy to manage, so let's start with geotagging, which is adding location data to the pictures you take.

- If you have an iPhone, from Settings you can go into Privacy and check Location Services to see if geotagging is turned on for your camera. If so, turn it off. While you're in Location Services, you can turn it off for other apps as well.

- For Android phones, the way you turn off geotagging varies from phone to phone depending on the camera application you use. However, you can open up your camera app and click on Settings where you can turn off the geotagging option.
- To remove geotag info from photo files on your Windows PC:
  1. In the folder that stores what you want to clean up, select a photo or group of photos, and then right-click.
  2. Click **Properties**, and then click **Details**.
  3. At the bottom of the window, click Remove Properties and Personal Information, and then click **OK**.
- To remove geotag info from photo files on your Mac:
  1. Double-click a photo to launch a preview of it.
  2. Press Command + I to launch **Inspector**.
  3. Select the "a" icon > GPS, and then click "Remove location info."

These directions may vary by device, manufacturer, and which operating system you're using, but the basics remain the same. If you have any issues, do a quick search on "remove metadata from photos," and include your device type and/or operating system. You'll find plenty of articles and videos that can walk you through it.

Protecting Your Baby's Identity

Just as you keep tabs on your identity (or should keep tabs on it, we'll catch up on that later), it's time to look after your baby's identity as well.

Let me start with something that might make you scratch your head: Freeze and monitor your baby's credit. No joke. Your baby has a name, an address, a date of birth, and a Social Security number (or the equivalent if you don't live in the U.S.), which are the key ingredients fraudsters need to obtain credit cards or pull off other fraudulent activities. It might not surprise you that there's a market out there for the Social Security numbers of babies. CNN reported on one such forum in 2018 where Social Security numbers of babies went for sale at the cost of $300 U.S. in Bitcoin.[11]

The info of babies is of much higher value to hackers because it often takes years for the breach to be discovered, such as when your child becomes old enough to get a job or apply for credit. It can even haunt them when they head in to get their first driver's license and find they have a couple hundred dollars of unpaid parking tickets racked up in their name.

How often is this happening? According to a Javelin Strategy & Research study in 2017, more than a million kids in the U.S. were victims, some 1.48% of the population. Some two-thirds of them were age 7 or younger.[12]

That's why it's important to monitor and freeze their credit now.

Placing a credit freeze is designed to prevent such fraud from happening and is now free in the U.S., thanks to a new law enacted in late 2018. Creating your freeze typically involves a phone call to each of the three major credit reporting agencies in the U.S. (Equifax, Experian, and TransUnion). And you'll receive a unique PIN to use when you want to lift it. A quick search on each of their websites will turn up a page on how you can get a free credit freeze going for your child.

Another thing to do when protecting your child's identity is to lock down your privacy settings on social media. According to Pew Research Center in 2018, nearly 70% of adults in the U.S. use some form of social media.[13] However, even as usage has climbed so have users' concerns about privacy, particularly about how those

---

[11] https://money.cnn.com/2018/01/22/technology/infant-data-dark-web-identity-theft/index.html

[12] https://www.cnbc.com/2018/04/24/child-identity-theft-is-a-growing-and-expensive-problem.html

[13] http://www.pewresearch.org/fact-tank/2018/03/27/americans-complicated-feelings-about-social-media-in-an-era-of-privacy-concerns/

platforms protect their information. A Pew Research Center survey conducted in 2016 found that:

... just 9% of social media users were "very confident" that social media companies would protect their data. About half of users were not at all or not too confident their data were in safe hands.

Note that things have changed since then. There's been tremendous pressure on social media executives from data privacy advocates and legislators in both the U.S. and the European Union (EU) has put new and reinforced regulations in place that make it easier for Europeans and people worldwide to have more insight into what data is being collected, how that data gets used, where it is stored, and how they can control it. Similar legislation is being considered in governments around the world.

Bringing this back to practical terms, one outcome of all this pressure is that it's getting easier for people to manage their privacy settings on social networks. Here's an example of what you can do right now by hopping into your Privacy settings in Facebook:

Privacy Settings and Tools

Your Activity	Who can see your future posts?	Friends	Edit
	Review all your posts and things you're tagged in		Use Activity Log
	Limit the audience for posts you've shared with friends of friends or Public?		Limit Past Posts
How People Find and Contact You	Who can send you friend requests?	Everyone	Edit
	Who can see your friends list?	Friends	Edit
	Who can look you up using the email address you provided?	Friends	Edit
	Who can look you up using the phone number you provided?	Friends	Edit
	Do you want search engines outside of Facebook to link to your profile?	No	Edit

Like all things digital, menus and the options within them change often. The important thing to look for right away is the option for who can see your posts (at the top in the illustration above). You'll want to set that to Friends (*not* Public). This helps ensure that only your friends will see what you post. Also, look toward the bottom of the menu to see that you can (and will want to) also bar search engines outside of Facebook (like Google or Bing) from including your data in search results. As I said earlier, this doesn't provide

100% assurance that people other than your friends will ever see your photos and posts, but it is absolutely the #1 best place to start.

I've already covered many of the plenty of reasons to lock down your social media profile and go private and "friends only." But here's an illustrative story from about 10 years ago about how a publicly posted pic can take a strange turn, which starts in Missouri, USA and ends up almost halfway around the world in eastern Europe.

Meet the Smith family of St. Louis. When it came time for a family portrait, they called upon a photographer friend who snapped the kind of shot people with small kids hope for. There they were, their family of four—mom, dad, and two preschoolers—each with beaming smiles. According to the story posted online in the *Guardian* in 2009,[14] they sent out the image with their holiday card, and Danielle, the family mom, posted it on her blog and a few other social media sites. Zip ahead a few months later to when another family friend was traveling in Prague, Czech Republic, and where a billboard stopped him in his proverbial tracks. There were the Smiths, apparently advertising a grocery store above a caption that translated to, "We will prepare and deliver your requests in two business days." (Wait, "two business days" to deliver prepared food? This is *clearly* 2009.) In the *Guardian* article, Danielle said of this turn of events and the internet fame that followed: "Interesting. Bizarre. Flattering, I suppose. But quite creepy."

A few things happened here. One is that this occurred a decade ago when privacy online was fast and loose. Without knowing which specific social media network(s) the picture was posted on or what privacy controls were available at that time, we can guess that these pictures were public. What's more, and innocently enough, especially back in 2009, Danielle posted a high-resolution quality version picture on her blog, which is exactly the type of image marketers need to make print ads that can go on billboards such as that Czech one. In the same article, she said she'd continue to post family pictures, but that they'd be low-resolution images.

---

[14] https://www.theguardian.com/media/2009/jun/11/smith-family-photo-czech-advertisement

Crazy, right? And that's one way we can show the difference between a "public" and "private" social media profile. So, ask yourself, is your family up for selling butter in Estonia? If not, lock up those privacy settings!

Another albeit darker instance of online identity theft occurs when people download pictures of other people's children and have them pose as their own. Yes, believe it or not that's a thing. At the time of writing this book, a news story making the rounds was of a toddler who looked super angry in a studio photo. Someone got a hold of the photo, posed as the toddler's dad online, and created a story about how the toddler was upset because he, "his dad," ate his Pop-Tart that morning. He went on to start a GoFundMe account to make sure "they" would never run out of Pop-Tarts.[15] There are other instances of people using a photo of a child to help their online dating chances. They feel having a cute child will endear them to someone. (I know, super creepy.)

Get Your Kiddo a Web Address

They're not just for the Kardashians anymore!

Securing a domain name for children gives them a piece of digital real estate they can eventually claim as their own one day. There are plenty of good reasons why your child should have his or her own dot-com, dot-net, or dot-whatever. The first is that you don't have to be famous to find it useful. With your own domain name purchased from a firm like GoDaddy or Wix, you can set up a custom email address or eventually host your own website on it if you wish. Second, it literally stakes your claim. Once you own it, no one else can use it, which provides another degree of control over your digital identity. Finally, it's inexpensive. Sure, dot-coms can sometimes get pricey, yet there are thousands of domains available beyond the classic dot-com and dot-net that provide inexpensive alternatives if the dot-com or dot-net you want is either taken or a little on the expensive side. Thing is, web domains are a finite

---

[15] https://www.wthr.com/article/little-boys-angry-school-photo-goes-viral-all-wrong-reasons

resource, which has given rise to domain name speculators who purchase domain names with the aim of selling it at a profit to an interested party somewhere down the road. Point being, now's the time to register your baby's domain name before someone else does.

What Did We Learn?

Let's pay another visit to your child's data lake. You'll see it's not quite a lake yet, but it's a rapidly expanding data puddle that's turning into a data pond. Think twice before you share. And I'll just say it: It pays to err hard on the side of caution. What goes on the internet is there forever. Importantly, give your kids a say. They have a moral right to veto power over what you do and do not post about them online. This starts in the preschool years, right around age 3, when they are gaining a sense of self, building friendships, and developing a sense of what's right and what's wrong. Your prudent use of social media can foster their healthy self-esteem. And in the meantime, when they're just infants and tots, be their defender. Hold their security and privacy in the highest possible regard. Take the time to manage it with the same intensity that you do your own. It will help establish a great foundation of trust that you can build on as they get older.

3

AGES 2 TO 10 – THE FORMATIVE YEARS

As our children toddle into their *terrible twos*, thus begins a struggle. Sure, it's easy to think of the terrible twos as *our* struggle as we're dealing with the tantrums, the stubbornness, or chasing a kiddo down the cereal aisle at the grocery store, wondering, "Why did we have kids again?" However, the real struggle is theirs. Kids in the throes of the terrible twos find themselves wrestling with two worlds—one of being entirely dependent on you and one of emerging independence. They're exploring. They're testing. They're pushing boundaries. (And your buttons!) As they go, they learn, and begin to carve out a vision of the world for themselves—with your guidance, of course, so that they can learn how to live a safe and happy life both now and as they get older.

It's no different with their digital world too.

Around age 2, kids get their first taste of playing on mommy or daddy's smartphone or tablet and discover an awesome new world of devices and online activities. It's slow at first—a couple of minutes here and there—but, over time, they spend more and more of their day online. According to Common Sense Media, children up to age 8 spend an average of 2 hours and 19 minutes every day on screen media. For kids 8 to 12, that figure grows to 4 hours and 36 minutes of screen time per day.[16] You have an opportunity when your child has their first experience with a connected device to set the tone for what's expected. Take a moment to pause here: this is a deliberate teaching moment, the first of many, where you explain how to go safely online and continue to reinforce these behaviors as they grow.

So, just as at home and in school, these are children's formative years in the digital world because there's a significant increase in their access to devices and online engagement—watching videos, playing games, interacting with educational software, and many other activities. Keeping them safe in this environment needs to be top of mind, and that includes awareness of how the data puddle that formed around the time they were born will rapidly become a data pond during these years. We need to be aware that this pond has direct ties to our privacy, their privacy, and, ultimately, to their life in general.

To help illustrate this point, how often do you go to a theater, an airport, or your local mall and see young children glued to a device? Those interactions are creating a groundswell of data that fills their burgeoning data lakes. Our smartphones and tablets have become what television was a generation ago—a babysitter for our kids. Except unlike a television, which was broadcasting in one direction, there is a lot of information going back and forth with our connected devices. You might know about some of it, like which sites are being accessed, but you might not be aware of other information being exchanged, such as location tracking.

Parenting with television was fairly easy in that it was pretty straightforward to make sure our children only watched certain stations or programs. Whereas with our connected devices, our kids are only a couple of clicks or taps away from an unfiltered plethora of virtually everything and anything we can imagine. So, without a doubt, there's a fair share for us to consider before we hand over our devices to our little ones.

---

[16] https://www.cnn.com/2017/11/15/health/screen-time-averages-parenting/index.html

Before I get too deep into this chapter it's important to note that I'm not suggesting this is necessarily a bad thing for children—especially if we set appropriate boundaries and teach them how to be safe online. However, I do believe that balance and moderation are the key to the development of a well-adjusted child. How you define that balance in your life depends on a number of factors specific to your household and beliefs. But suffice it to say that thoroughly thinking through this with your child's digital well-being hanging in the balance would be a great use of your time. And with the inevitable changes you, your family, and your child will experience, you'll need to regularly reconsider the criteria you use for establishing that balance.

The Importance of Rules

As reported in the Role Modeling section of parentandteen.com (website of the Center for Parent and Teen Communication), "Modeling safe behavior is necessary to raise children who will use their devices appropriately. In her book, *Media Moms & Digital Dads: A Fact-Not-Fear Approach to Parenting in the Digital Age*, Yalda Uhls explains, 'Every adult who wants to help children navigate the digital world should consider carefully his own media behavior.'"[17]

There it is. The old parenting adage: "Do as I say, not as I do." Your children are watching, and in many cases mimicking, everything you do both online and offline. They're absorbing your interactions with devices and the world in general like a sponge. This is where you can set an example of what good online behaviors and habits look like. If they see you looking at your phone while eating dinner with the family or distracted by your device while driving your car, they will think this is OK despite you saying otherwise. Likewise, if they see you spending time with the family on a slow Saturday afternoon instead of poking around idly on your phone, or biding time patiently while waiting for an appointment without staring at your device the entire time, you will reinforce positive habits that will likely last a lifetime.

---

[17] https://parentandteen.com/being-a-role-model-in-the-digital-age/

As to what that balance looks like to you, that's for you to determine because there aren't any absolute answers here. However, common sense and common courtesy are the rules of thumb. For example, watching a couple movies on a long car ride is probably just fine—but firing up the phone during their older sister's cello recital certainly isn't. (And if you think the cello recital example is a bit extreme, think again. I've seen it happen all the time.)

Establishing and reinforcing rules is paramount in these formative years. Of course, some of those rules are relatively easy to discuss and enforce. You can set the amount of time your child can be online, and you can establish a time when all screens are turned off. You can also set rules around the *places* where they can go online—like at home versus while shopping at the supermarket. Yet, as I'm sure you know, children grow into master negotiators. You'll see them start developing those negotiating skills in earnest, particularly as they get hooked on devices. They might even present any good deed as a means to garner more screen time. And that's fine. Be consistent and leave room for rewards and "special occasions" too. Think of how you moderate your own time, and how you give yourself little "rewards" of screen time. Thinking along those lines will help you build rules for your children.

However, if you're looking for some hard and fast guidance, the U.S. Department of Agriculture recommended in 2013 that children under 2 years of age should not be in front of a screen at all, and over that age the maximum leisure screen time should be no more than two hours a day.[18] Meanwhile, the American Academy of Pediatrics recommends children ages 2 to 5 be limited to one hour of screen time a day, with consistent limits for older children on the amount of time and place they get to have screen time.[19] While the specifics differ, the heart of the guidance remains consistent—keep the amount of screen time limited, and further limit it to specific times and places for kids to go online. The reason for this is that apps, even the apps that are marketed as educational apps, are no substitute for non-screen activities and good old interaction with

---

[18] https://fns-prod.azureedge.net/sites/default/files/limitscreen.pdf
[19] https://www.heart.org/en/news/2018/08/06/limit-screen-time-among-kids-experts-caution

others. There's plenty of research on the topic, and I encourage you to take a little time to do your own research online and to figure out what works best for your family. One place you can start is Common Sense Media, which is packed with resources. Their editors carefully comb all manner of media, from books and movies to TV shows and apps, and provide ratings and reviews that help parents make choices about what content and what messages their kids are exposed to. Drop by their app section, where they have an entire category dedicated to preschoolers, along with other categories for older kids too.

Online Etiquette for Children

Just as important, but more difficult for children to understand, are the rules of etiquette—the finer points of how we treat people, handle different situations, and simply get around in the world. What makes teaching those rules a little more challenging to impart is the "why." Why do we say "please" and "thank you" when we're at the dinner table? Why do we look people in the eye when we talk to them? Really, a large part of it comes down to being a thoughtful and caring individual. So the digital age requires us to teach our children rules of online etiquette, including the importance of soft skills such as empathy and compassion. They must learn that behind those pictures and words on the screen are other people who have their own emotions and feelings that need to be considered.

Our online rules need to include expectations for our children's conduct during online interactions with others. There are powerful values we should teach our children about their behavior online. I came across some common-sense rules on the Verywell Family website and loved what I read:

Treat Others How You Want to Be Treated
Almost everyone is familiar with the "golden rule." But sometimes kids need to be reminded of the importance of good manners, even online. Remind them that it is always best to discuss sensitive or potentially volatile issues with the person directly rather than posting something online or sending a hurtful e-mail. Also, discuss what a healthy friendship looks like and be sure they know this applies to online communication as well.

Keep Messages and Posts Positive and Truthful

Encourage kids to censor their messages and posts to be sure they are not sarcastic, negative or rude. They also should avoid posting anything that is not true such as rumors or gossip. Kids also should know what cyberbullying is and that they should never engage in that type of behavior. Meanwhile, if they are being victimized, make sure they know how to respond to cyberbullying.

Double-Check Messages Before Hitting Send

Teaching kids to slow down and think about their posts, comments, texts, and e-mails is crucial. They need to realize that once they press send, there is no way to take back their words. Even if they delete a post later, it still can remain available for others to see especially if someone took a screenshot. Encourage them to always read their messages, comments, and posts several times to see if they could be misinterpreted or if they come off sarcastic.

Kids also need to realize that being funny online is very hard to accomplish. The person on the other end cannot see their facial expressions or hear their tone of voice. Sometimes a message that is meant to be funny does not come off that way at all. As a general rule, they should avoid making jokes online.

Do Not Violate a Friend's Confidence

Today's world is saturated with photos, texts and videos that can be posted, copied, forwarded, downloaded and altered in a matter of minutes. Encourage your kids to ask themselves how they would feel if one of their most embarrassing moments was put on display for the world to see.

Remind your kids to think about what they are about to post. They should ask themselves the following questions: Did my friends tell me this in confidence? Will it embarrass them? Will sharing this information compromise their privacy or stir up drama? If they answer yes to any of those questions, they should keep the information to themselves. After all, that is what a good friend would do. Another good rule of thumb is to always ask permission before posting a picture of someone.[20]

These are great foundational rules, but you should consider other rules that may be more appropriate for your family or situation.

---

[20] https://www.verywellfamily.com/things-to-teach-your-kids-about-digital-etiquette-460548

Parental Controls

You're not always going to be able to look over your kiddo's shoulder while they're online. Applying parental controls is one way to prevent them from experiencing things that they shouldn't or going places that you don't want them to. These controls are basically digital rules, where technology does part of the work by governing your child's online activities. What are they exactly? Wikipedia has a pretty good definition:

Parental controls are features which may be included in digital television services, computer and video games, mobile devices and software that allow parents to restrict the access of content to their children. These controls were created to assist parents in their ability to restrict certain content viewable by their children ... Parental controls fall into roughly four categories: content filters, which limit access to age inappropriate content; usage controls, which constrain the usage of these devices such as placing time-limits on usage or forbidding certain types of usage; computer usage management tools, which enforces the use of certain software; and monitoring, which can track location and activity when using the devices.[21]

There are several software vendors that create parental control software. Most offer the ability to have the software installed on all major operating systems, including PCs, Macs, and all kinds of mobile devices. Plenty of them do a lot of work for you by providing you with pre-populated "blacklists" of sites and content types that you can immediately restrict, typically based upon specific age ranges. Some other useful capabilities include features like geofencing that will inform you if your child strays outside a defined area and social media monitoring to keep tabs on their posts and activities. Also, check to see if your internet router offers parental controls—some manufacturers include that functionality in the device, at the source of your home internet. They can often be somewhat difficult to use, but they might suffice if you're a more tech-savvy person.

You should consider your specific needs and research the one that works best for you. Whichever route you go, I suggest you put

---

[21] https://en.wikipedia.org/wiki/Parental_controls

parental controls in place as part of an ongoing dialogue with your child. Only through constant communications can you hope to connect with your child to safely navigate this new digital world. Talk about why those controls are in place. Talk about what does and does not work for your family. And talk about what's age-appropriate content and what's not. Just as movies and games have their rating system, your family has one of its own too. Make that clear.

Here's another way to think about parental controls: the internet is the biggest neighborhood there is. Just as you give your kids more and more freedom to roam about your actual neighborhood as they get older, more capable, and more aware, you can take the same approach to opening up and closing off portions of their digital world. Parental controls give you the tools to do exactly that. For your laptop or home computer, you can also set up a separate profile for your kids that limits what apps they can use.

For smaller kidlets, there's even more you can do: There are numerous "play zone" apps that allow them access on a parent's phone to only kid-appropriate content in a secure garden of sorts. We sometimes refer to these secure gardens as sandboxes in that they provide a controlled environment that prevents those in a them from straying into other areas.[22] One example from the UK and the BBC iPlayer Kids offers nothing but commercial-free shows for little ones. There's also the Kiddle browser by Google (www.kiddle.co). Per Google, "Kiddle is a visual search engine for kids powered by Google, offering safe kids web, image, and video search. Results are vetted by editors."

Conscientious and smart folks continue to roll out solutions for controlling what your children are exposed to—often in ways that feel friendly (and not heavy-handed). There are plenty more examples of apps that will cordon off internet areas you don't want them exploring but will still give them the joys and benefits of life online. I encourage you to hop online and do a few searches for "kids apps" or "best apps for kids." My bet is that you'll be pleasantly surprised by how many good ones you'll find.

---

[22] https://en.wikipedia.org/wiki/Sandbox_(computer_security)

Cyberbullying (Part One)

An important consideration during the formative years is understanding what safe online interactions generally look like for children. As a new parent, you may hear the term "cyberbullying" being thrown around from time to time. But what exactly is cyberbullying, and what does it look like? According to StopBullying.gov:

Cyberbullying is bullying that takes place over digital devices like cell phones, computers, and tablets. Cyberbullying can occur through SMS, Text, and apps, or online in social media, forums, or gaming where people can view, participate in, or share content. Cyberbullying includes sending, posting, or sharing negative, harmful, false, or mean content about someone else. It can include sharing personal or private information about someone else causing embarrassment or humiliation. Some cyberbullying crosses the line into unlawful or criminal behavior. [23]

From there, the site goes on to explain the most common places cyberbullying occurs:

- *Social media, such as Facebook, Instagram, Snapchat, and Twitter.*
- *SMS (Short Message Service) also known as text messages sent through devices.*
- *Instant messages (via devices, email provider services, apps, and social media messaging features).*
- *Email* [24]

When you scan that list, you'll quickly see that these aren't places little ones go when they are just starting their online journey. But you know that soon enough they will be immersed in the world of text messages, social media, and the like to interact directly with family members, friends, or other children. So, these formative years are a good time for you to carefully consider when your kids should have access to such experiences in the first place.

---

[23] https://www.stopbullying.gov/
[24] Ibid.

It's important for you to know and look for signs that your child is being bullied online. Chances are, if it's happening, they won't tell you because they might not feel comfortable sharing what they are going through. According to Understood.org, signs that cyberbullying might be happening can include when your child:

- *Suddenly stops using the computer, even though he's always enjoyed it before.*
- *Doesn't want to use the computer in a place where you can see it.*
- *Turns off the computer monitor or changes screens every time you walk by.*
- *Seems nervous or jumpy when he gets an instant message, text, or email.*
- *Alludes to bullying indirectly by saying something like, "There's a lot of drama at school," or "I have no friends."*
- *Doesn't want to go to school or appears uneasy about going.*
- *Becomes withdrawn.*[25]

If you notice your child exhibiting any of these signs, ease into a discussion about what they are experiencing. Keep in mind that this is a deeply impactful situation that they are struggling to comprehend. Understood.org goes on to say:

Start by talking to your child. You can open the conversation by describing a bullying incident that happened to you as a child, or an example of cyberbullying that you heard about on the news. If your child isn't forthcoming, calmly tell him that you're going to exercise your right to be the administrator of his computer and phone. You need to be able to see where he's been online and the history of what he's deleted.

If you confirm that he is being bullied, there are things you can do to put a stop to it. Suggest to your child that he let the bullies know you have access to his electronics: "I know this sounds crazy, but my parents are the administrators of this computer so they can see everything. I can't control what they do."

---

[25] https://www.understood.org/en/friends-feelings/child-social-situations/online-activities-social-media/how-to-tell-if-your-child-is-being-bullied-online

If that doesn't work and the bullying is intense and frequent, you may need to take one or all of these three steps:

- *Talk to the parents of the kids who are bullying your child. Let them know what's going on and how it's affecting him.*
- *Reach out to your child's guidance counselor or principal. Every school should have anti-cyberbullying policies and protocols to help.*
- *If neither of those strategies works, you may need to get law enforcement involved. Print out or save evidence of the bullying in case you need it to show the police.[26]*

I can't stress this enough: Take cyberbullying seriously. Any bullying is harmful, but the online variety can be particularly noxious—especially if it's out there for all the world to see and pile on because it's posted in a public space like a social media account. Think of how horrific that behavior would be to an adult such as yourself; now think of how utterly damaging it would be for a young child who's still forming a sense of who they are in the world. If you even suspect that this is happening to your child, or someone else's child, act on it. In the next chapter, we'll cover cyberbullying in even more detail, with a candid look at how it can impact tweens, teens, and their families. In the meantime, know that you'll want to broach the topic (and keep an eye out for cyberbullying) as your child gets further into the grade school years. These behaviors begin to take root at this age, and their effects are felt both in and out of school.

The Talk (Well, perhaps not *the* talk but an important talk nonetheless.)

Explaining online risks and threats without scaring the bejeebers out of full-grown adults is tough enough. Doing so with a kid is orders of magnitude tougher. Yet do it we must.

Explaining these things to a young child can be daunting because you need to have a firm grasp on what they are and because you want to strike a balance with the multitude of benefits derived from being online. Tone is massively important because you don't want to scare kids, but they do need to understand the consequences should they

---

[26] Ibid.

inadvertently find themselves mixed up in some malicious activity, inappropriate social circumstances, or worse.

I've always leaned into humor to help explain these types of topics to my kids, but you should assess what approach you're comfortable with and be prepared to answer some difficult questions. The important thing is building up the moxie to have the discussion. You can start by telling them that most people they will interact with online are honest and have good intentions, but some people are dishonest and will have bad intentions of harming them or their family members.

Because of this you need to help them understand that these bad people use a variety of techniques in an attempt to influence them to do their bidding. (What starts as a very innocuous interaction could rapidly spiral into a full-blown crisis.) It's important to encourage your kids to ask you before taking any actions online such as clicking on an advertisement or downloading an application, and to come to you when they're uncertain about what they're seeing or what a website (or person!) is asking them to do. A young child may struggle to understand the nuances of this, so a way to sum it up is to explain that they should not do things online that they wouldn't do in the offline world.

For example, we teach our kids not to talk to strangers. The same is true for strangers online. Your child should not accept any type of invitation from anyone or otherwise engage with anyone who you do not know. If they're being asked for personal information, like their phone number or home address, they need to know not to give it—and to tell a parent or guardian when it happens. Your child may feel it's not a big deal to accept a friend request from a stranger that appears to be legit since there's an implied distance. In their mind, it's not as if they are showing up at your door trying to gain access to your home and family. However, some of those people are doing just that, albeit digitally. Those strangers looking to access and influence your child are referred to as cyber predators.

According to *Cyber Safety*, "Cyber predators are people who use the internet to exploit usually younger people for sexual and other purposes. Many cyber predators pretend to be someone else or lie about details about themselves to gain trust of their victims. It has been estimated that *one in five* children have been sexually solicited online."[27]

You may be asking yourself what the difference is between a cyber predator and a cyberstalker. I'll cover cyberstalking in the next chapter because it generally starts to manifest more in the 11 to 17 age range.

There are several topics about being online that you will need to discuss with your child. I can't stress strongly enough the importance of maintaining a balanced and moderate tone and not being accusatory when having these discussions: your child will more likely absorb and respect your words and point of view as they start to spend time online when you're not in the immediate vicinity. So when it's time to have what we'll call the "cyber talk," here's a list of items you should cover:

- We all talk with our children about the importance of sharing. But when it comes to sharing information online, explain to them that they should not share items like their full name, address, telephone number, or other personal items without your approval.
- Your child will want to share specifics of activities you are planning. You should encourage them to share the experience *after* it has happened instead of sharing plans in advance—and have them show you what they plan on sharing before it gets posted.
- This is a great time to teach good password hygiene. Explain to your child to use passwords with letters and numbers and to not use names of family members or other family identifiers such as your pet's name. Make sure your child knows they need to tell you the sites and applications they use that require a username and password and to share with you what those username and passwords are.

---

[27] http://cybersafetyed.weebly.com/cyber-predators.html

- Encourage them to ask you before sharing photos. Your child may not understand the full extent of information contained in photos, such as your street address, school name, or license plate number.

- Likewise, have them ask you before installing any applications or joining any online forums or social media sites. You should be sure to read reviews about what they are asking you to do and make sure any app your child wants to download is age appropriate.

- As they start to join social media sites, make sure that you have access to their accounts and regularly monitor who they are having discussions with and the context of those discussions. If anyone shows up that you don't personally know, be prepared to block them and have a discussion with your child about who they are. The discussion shouldn't be filled with tension. It's important that you remain calm and composed. Remember they are just now navigating the nuances of appropriate online behaviors, so the conversation should revolve around the importance of bridging physical friendships with those online.

- Regularly check the privacy settings on the sites that your child frequents. I would encourage very aggressive privacy settings early on that can be throttled back as your child learns how to be safe online. (This applies to the parental controls I talked about earlier in this chapter as well. Start tight, then ease up, having discussions with your child along the way.)

- Kids tend to be click happy: they will click on almost anything put in front of them. This can have devastating consequences—from installing malware on your device to giving cybercriminals access to your credit card information. As your child starts to interact with your devices, work closely with them to explain how they should pause and think before clicking on items that appear on-screen. (We'll cover more about this later in the book because you'd be surprised how sophisticated some of these "phishing" attacks can get. Adults often fall for them, even when they're doing their best to be wary!)

I understand if you feel the list above may seem a bit heavy-handed and that you should trust your child to make the right decisions. Some might even view some items as outright violations of their child's privacy. I would tend to agree if it weren't for the stark reality that there are a lot of really bad people constantly trolling on the lookout to take advantage of an unsuspecting child.

I had the opportunity to meet a wonderful young lady, Alicia Kozakiewicz,[28] at an online safety for children event at an elementary school in Colorado. Her story reflects the true horror that comes from engaging in a discussion with a stranger online. From her website:

In January of 2002, Alicia Kozakiewicz became the victim of an Internet luring and was abducted to another state where she was held captive. Following a miraculous rescue by the FBI, Alicia, still recovering from her ordeal, returned to school and was soon highly involved in both academic and extracurricular activities, graduating with high honors. During these years, she came to realize that other children need not suffer her traumatic experience, and so, "The Alicia Project," Internet safety and awareness education, was born.

Fortunately, Alicia is a survivor who now educates children, individuals and organizations around the world about just how susceptible children can be and actively promotes online safety for children. Unfortunately, her story is not an isolated incident. It happens all too often. Having a regular, healthy dialogue with your children about who they are interacting with online and what they are doing is a crucial part of keeping your child safe.

How Screen Time Impacts Children

Another important aspect of being online that I think more parents are beginning to recognize, to some degree, is that extended screen time causes behavioral and other important developmental disorders in young children. This recognition should be advanced in the face of sobering statistics such as those from a long-term study in France highlighted in an article on Aleteia.org:

---

[28] http://www.aliciaproject.org/

The National Education department published its benchmarks and statistical references for 2018, including the number of school children who are suffering from some variety of cognitive handicap. "The results are striking," laments a representative of CoSE. "The number of children between the ages of 2 and 11 suffering from intellectual and cognitive problems, psychological problems, and language disorders is increasing dramatically. Since 2010, cases of intellectual and cognitive disorders have increased by 24 percent, psychological disorders by 54 percent, and speech and language disorders by 94 percent." In the space of 10 years, children have developed more and more difficulty expressing themselves, learning, and managing their emotions.[29]

This is just the latest research in what has been well documented for years and is only getting worse. Studies from various countries all suggest that children are getting too much exposure to screens, including television, computers, tablets, and phones, and that such exposure is having long-term consequences. Suffice it to say that we as parents must actively pursue healthy alternatives to plopping our kids in front of a screen when they appear to be or complain about being bored.

Gaming and the Young Gamer

Ah yes, the inevitable topic: online gaming! I know some of you have alarm bells going off in your heads as you reel from all the horror stories of children suffering from sloth-like malaise as they immerse themselves in online competitions. As I write this, the veritable poster-child for the highs and lows of online gaming is *Fortnite*. It's a cartoony battle royale game loaded with guns, vehicles, shield potions, and crazy character get-ups called "skins" that has kids (of all ages) rapt in hours of online play. Of course, we're talking about the formative years right now, but this is when games like this start to hit children's radar—even more so if they have older siblings.

A child's first exposure to gaming on a device may be through gaming apps on your smartphone or tablet to serve as a distraction while you focus on something else that needs tending to, or it may be through educational software that uses gamification techniques

---

[29] https://aleteia.org/2019/02/09/early-screen-exposure-linked-to-cognitive-and-developmental-problems-in-children/

to retain interest in a subject. Either way, gaming will likely be an online activity that your child is drawn to. The time is now to set expectations and strike balances between gaming online and other activities, both online and offline.

For starters, I strongly suggest that you pay close attention to age-appropriate games. Carefully read the descriptions and look for labeling on the package that gives age and content guidance. Also give screenshots or demo videos a look—many games in online stores have them. Taking some time to review a game your child wants will tell you a great deal. Don't give your consent and download away just because it's convenient. (Earlier in chapter 1, I mentioned Common Sense Media as a resource for finding age-appropriate apps. They're great for identifying age-appropriate games as well.)

I've seen many of my friends with younger kids simply sit down and watch them play. This is highly instructive! One, it can reassure you that what they're playing is indeed fine for their age, and two, it can lead to plenty of teaching moments. After all, games are about rules, structure, winning, losing, and how to deal with how all those things come together. Thus, the best games can impart little life lessons—like learning what makes a good winner or how not to be a sore loser. What's more, playing games with your kid or spending some time alongside them as they play on their own opens up other opportunities to teach them about online etiquette, such as how to handle chat requests (or comments) from other players when they are older and playing online games. (And we'll talk about that in more detail in the next chapter because voice and text chatting in video games really take off during the tween and teen years.) Bottom line: nothing beats your eagle eye when it comes to making sure your kid is in a good place with games they play and how they play them.

To be clear, I am in no way advocating that you throw your hands up and let your child game to their heart's content. As I mentioned at the onset of this chapter, determining what makes sense for you and your child should be very deliberate and balanced based on your specific aspirations and lifestyle and with the appropriate rules and boundaries well understood.

One thing that's not often discussed are the *benefits* of gaming as part of an overall healthy mix of activities. An article by Dr. Becky Parry, lecturer in digital literacies at the University of Sheffield, outlines twelve reasons why playing video games can be good for your children.[30] (Check out the link in the footnote; it's worth the full read.) One striking reason is how some video games can provide positive role models for girls and encourage their interest in Science, Technology, Engineering, and Math (STEM) subjects. There are games that incorporate analytical thinking through puzzles and pattern recognition, and there are apps that let kids tell their own stories or design video games of their own. Again, you point them in the right direction, and a little search time online can uncover lists and blogs dedicated to showcasing some of the more outstanding games.

A point that really struck with me from Dr. Parry's article—and perhaps it's no mistake that she saved this item for last—is that the online world and the "real" world can easily co-exist:

Online vs Offline
Video game play and active play don't have to be two separate things. Research highlights the way children adopt ideas from games in their physical play in the garden, on their bikes and even on the trampoline. This might come in useful when you think it's time for a break. You could suggest a related offline activity—such as creating a Fortnite diary or inventing a new Pokémon.

When I read that bit about inventing new Pokémon characters— the little critters who populate that game—I got a big smile on my face. A few years back, a friend of mine had about a half-dozen Pokémon that he'd created with his kids posted on his fridge with magnets. It was wonderful. With crayons and paper, the new world and the old came together, all while providing some welcome time away from screens. And another note about Pokémon; I'd be remiss if I didn't mention the *Pokémon Go* craze of not long ago where you'd see families running about parks as they hunted down digital Pokémon critters with their smartphones in real-world locations. A

---

[30] https://theconversation.com/twelve-reasons-to-let-your-children-play-video-games-this-christmas-108366

video game actually getting families outside and spending time together? Fantastic.

In all, when it comes to gaming, finding balance is key—and part of that is realizing that online games and the outside world aren't necessarily at odds with each other.

Your Role in a Growing Data Lake

Hey, remember all those baby pictures and videos you took? They keep adding up. From little moments to life events, your child's digital chronicle or footprint continues to grow. As those photos, videos, stories, and more are captured, stored, and shared like never before, you have your hands on the pump that directs data into your child's data pond. A great way to throttle the flood of data is really thinking through what should be broadcast via social media or shared more privately via email or text messaging. Our first impulse it to share these events broadly. Just as we talked about in the last chapter, think twice before posting and lock down the floodgates instead of manning the pump.

Every year as our children grow, adorable things happen that we want to share with our family and friends through social media along with other applications and technologies. The first day of school, a trip to the zoo, or donning Halloween costumes as they prepare to embark on a festive evening of trick-or-treating are all great examples of shareable moments. And since most of us now carry the equivalent of a high-powered digital SLR camera in our back pockets or purses, we're able to capture and share those special moments in real time, as they happen. You will feel compelled to generously post all these photos and provide a rich narrative of the circumstances surrounding them. This is where you should exercise caution in a couple of regards.

- First, the broader stroke is that those with malicious intent can build a profile that can be used to target you and your family now or in the future. That first-day-of-school picture will pinpoint where your kid goes to grade school. That vacation photo of the family doing cannonballs in the pool lets people know you're on vacation in the Poconos right now. That photo of the kids in front of the new car captures your license plate number. And so on. I'm not trying to tell you that the world is out to get you, but if there's no good reason to expose that kind of information about you and your family, why do it?

- The second is the permanence of what's posted. You should consider how your child will feel when they fully understand the circumstances surrounding the postings and the potential of them being very embarrassed or feeling betrayed. What seems like a light-hearted photo and description today could very well have real consequences for your children later in life. We talked about this earlier in the book, and the same applies here—particularly as they get older and should have some say into what you do and do not post about them.

What Did We Learn?

As you think about what approaches you can take to keep your children safe as they first take guarded and then increasingly independent steps online, consider the following:

- Have discussions early and often with your children on how to be safe online. Setting the tone for this early will help ensure a lifetime of good habits. If you're a bit unsure or overwhelmed about what that entails, review the various resources outlined in this chapter.
- Talk to your school and make sure they have a curriculum that educates students on being safe online. If they don't, a little online research will uncover organizations and resources that can help.
- Use sandboxing and parental control software to help set time limits and boundaries for your children.
- Establish a healthy balance of screen time and other activities.
- Regularly monitor who your children are communicating with online and what sites they are spending time on.
- Spend time with your kids alongside or nearby them when they're online. See what games they're playing, and know

who and what they're spending their time with—parental controls, as good as they are, aren't a substitute for your supervision and care.

- If you're at all concerned that your child is being bullied online or you see any indications that someone else's child is being bullied, don't hesitate to act on those concerns— taking steps as recommended earlier in this chapter.

I can't stress strongly enough the importance of this chapter. If you commit to building the right online skills and behaviors during the formative years, both in what you say and what you do, your child will likely enjoy a lifetime of safe online experiences. That's not to say that bad things won't happen, but if they do your child will be armed with how to deal with the adversity.

A big part of building those skills and behaviors is to encourage your children to ask you questions about what they are experiencing online. You may not always have the answer, but there are ample resources you can look to that will help you frame a discussion about the challenges they are facing. A few resources to help get you get and stay educated and informed include the following:

- The National Cybersecurity Alliance
  https://staysafeonline.org/
- Internet Matters https://www.internetmatters.org/
- Childnet International https://www.childnet.com/
- McAfee Family Safety blogs
  https://securingtomorrow.mcafee.com/category/consum
  er/family-safety/

You can also reach out to school counselors, members of your church, extended family members, or other trusted members of your community. The important thing is to find the answers so you can keep the dialogue moving with your child.

4

AGES 11 TO 17 – FROM TWEENS TO TEENS

For anyone who asks what happens during the tween through teen years, the best answer is probably what *doesn't* happen?

Just so you know, I've been there; done that; got the T-shirt. And I survived. Albeit barely it feels! My kids were the first generation to grow up on social media. Like most teens in the mid-2000's, they got their first taste with MySpace and then switched to Facebook as the masses made the shift there around 2009. They also got into other platforms like Instagram and stuck with them while others came and went. And yes, there were plenty of challenges from sharing almost every facet of their lives. I won't get into details here as it might embarrass my kids but suffice it to say that mistakes were made.

Being a security and privacy practitioner, I made sure there were lots of discussions on how to use these platforms safely. The early discussions centered on privacy and the permanence of data and then blended into security as the platforms were leveraged with scams and other malicious activities. As you can imagine, when they were tweens and teens, the internet was a different place than it is today.

Of course, that's the nature of the internet. It's growing and changing as a greater and greater percentage of people in the world become connected. Internet connectivity has become as important as water and power in most homes. In 2018, that number was 55.1%, more than doubling in a decade.[31] What's more, that figure doesn't account for the internet of things (IoT)—the term used to describe the connected *things* on the internet (home alarm systems, thermostats, light bulbs, cameras, smart utility meters), a figure that grows as connectivity is being built into more and more devices because plenty of once mundane devices are now getting connected to the internet. Estimates vary, yet projections point to 31 *billion* connected devices on the internet by 2020—close to four IoT devices per person in the world. Today, we connect about 4,800 new devices every minute of every day. IDC predicts that by 2025 we will be connecting 152,000 new things every minute of every day.

Whoa.

Just How Big Is Their Digital World?

So, today's internet is a bigger place that offers more commerce, entertainment, and avenues of communication than ever before. It's also a more complex place that presents the danger of more dark corners than ever before. The evolution of its characteristics will continue apace, which arguably introduces equal degrees of excitement and uncertainty about the shape it will take next. This is the digital world your teen is stepping into right now. It's no surprise that the matters of privacy and online safety have become bigger and more complex as well.

Let's take a look back a good fifteen or so years ago to when my kids were teens and what I had to concern myself when it came to their internet usage: Social media was becoming all the rage, and with new platforms jockeying for as many users as possible there was very little regard for security or privacy. Because the first generation of smartphones offered very limited plans for data, calls, and messaging, they needed to be closely monitored. I recall receiving several outrageous phone bills due to my kids texting. Most of our

---

[31] https://www.internetworldstats.com/emarketing.htm

online activities took place on the "home" PC with the biggest challenge being who got to use it when. We also kept one in the kitchen to ensure we could watch how it was being used.

Today's internet usage is primarily mobile. Smartphones are getting more powerful and ubiquitous every year, as are the apps we use on them. In fact, mobile apps accounted for nearly half of all traffic on the internet in 2017.[32] Amidst all of that usage, social media apps dominate the most frequently used apps (39%), while gaming and communication and messaging apps tie for second (10%), this according to a survey published by The Manifest in 2018.[33] However, the study cites an important caveat—app users are probably underreporting how often they use apps, likely because they struggle to estimate their own behavior.

Put another way, hopping on an app, such as one of your social media accounts, is something you do without even thinking about it anymore. One moment you're standing in the Target checkout line, and the next you're on your phone flipping through your feed when you suddenly catch yourself and think, "Heavens to Murgatroyd, how in the heck did I end up here?" Because of this, we can also say that internet usage is persistent. The internet is always with us, at our side, because our phones are too. And we do like our phones!

A mobile and persistent internet … that describes teen internet usage pretty well, doesn't it? Pardon any sappiness on my part here, but there was a time we put our kids to bed with their teddy bears. Now, as teens, they put themselves to bed with their phones—and wake up next to them too. Then there's the number of hours teens spend with them each day, nine on average according to a study published by Common Sense Media in 2015. That's an absolute gush of data they're generating each day.

While it's difficult to nail down the average amount of data one person creates, we can look at what happens in an "Internet Minute"

---

[32] https://www.statista.com/topics/779/mobile-internet/
[33] https://themanifest.com/app-development/mobile-app-usage-statistics-2018

thanks to an annual snapshot of online activity provided by Cumulus Media in 2017:

- 16 million text messages
- 2.5 million "Snap" messages in Snapchat
- 156 million emails sent
- 3.5 million searches on Google
- 900,000 logins on Facebook
- 4.1 million YouTube videos viewed[34]

That was 2017, and the numbers have only gone up because of a growing internet user base and an increased appetite for content and interaction. Granted, these figures reflect all usage across all users, not just teens, but they illustrate a point: When teens are diving into this vast and growing internet for nine hours a day on average, that activity begs a closer look by you and by your teen as well. With every Snapchat they send, every photo they post on Instagram, and all the shows they watch on streaming accounts, their data pond is quickly becoming a full-blown lake.

Also consider that today we consume, on average, 650 megabytes of data every day. Think of how much you stream music and your favorite Netflix shows and of the seemingly countless number of text messages your teen sends. By 2020 that number will skyrocket to 1.5 gigabytes of data as our thirst for data consumption grows and as the volume of connected things increases.

The Effects of All That Screen Time

Although this is a book on digital safety and privacy, it's ultimately a book about the well-being of you and your family, so I want to touch on a topic that has a growing body of research behind it: the physical and emotional effects of screen time on teens. And really, when you get down to it, this topic affects us all.

---

[34] https://www.weforum.org/agenda/2017/08/what-happens-in-an-internet-minute-in-2017

The year 2017 marked a first for research about cell phone usage and teens. The journal *Child Development* published a study that made a direct connection between screen time and mental health. Specifically, it showed that teens' usage of their phones late at night leads to disrupted sleep which in turn leads to increased rates of depression. A few culprits are cited. One is the simple fact that teens are up and on the phone instead of calling it a night. Also, screen light suppresses the secretion of melatonin and disrupts their circadian rhythm, both of which are important for proper sleep. Any light will do this at night, but blue light (like from a screen) acts most powerfully in that regard. Finally, the content they're either creating or consuming may stimulate their brains into a more active state.

In recent years, we've seen some phone manufacturers add in a "nighttime mode" that switches the screen's color scheme from a blue to a more sepia tone. That might be an improvement, but Harvard Medical School reports that:

> *Even dim light can interfere with a person's circadian rhythm and melatonin secretion. A mere eight lux—a level of brightness exceeded by most table lamps and about twice that of a night light—has an effect, notes Stephen Lockley, a Harvard sleep researcher. Light at night is part of the reason so many people don't get enough sleep, says Lockley, and researchers have linked short sleep to increased risk for depression, as well as diabetes and cardiovascular problems.*[35]

Maybe we could simply give our tweens and teens a bedtime teddy bear? Okay, no. But we would all do well to heed additional advice from the experts at Harvard Medical School:

- Avoid looking at bright screens beginning two to three hours before bed.
- If you work a night shift or use a lot of electronic devices at night, consider wearing blue-blocking glasses or installing an app that filters the blue/green wavelength at night.

---

[35] https://www.health.harvard.edu/staying-healthy/blue-light-has-a-dark-side

- Expose yourself to lots of bright light during the day, which will boost your ability to sleep at night, as well as your mood and alertness during daylight.[36]

And then there's my bit of advice: use that "nighttime mode" on your phone or tablet—or even better, turn the devices off and opt for a good night's sleep.

Besides blue light from screens at and around bedtime, there are other aspects of our digital world that can have an effect on the health of your teen (and your health as well—all of this advice goes for you too). These include the following concerns:

- Increased indoor time also means less exposure to sunlight, which might explain studies that have shown our vitamin D levels have been diminishing over the years. Vitamin D, known as the sunshine vitamin, is important for developing strong bones. Low levels of vitamin D have been associated with health consequences such as increased risk of death from cardiovascular disease, cognitive impairment in older adults, severe asthma in children, and cancer.[37]
- Outcomes associated with a more sedentary lifestyle— increased screen time and decreased physical activity—can include obesity, diabetes, cardiovascular disease, and even certain types of cancers.[38]
- There appears to be increasing evidence of pathways between social media usage and depression and that depressed teens tend to use social media more. "Countless studies have found a link between overuse of social media and decreased mental health. For instance, according to a study published in the Journal of Social and Clinical Psychology, study participants who limited their use of Facebook, Instagram and Snapchat reported significantly

---

[36] Ibid.
[37] https://www.webmd.com/diet/guide/vitamin-d-deficiency#1
[38] Ibid.

reduced levels of loneliness and depression, compared with participants who used social media without limits."[39]

These topics fall somewhat outside our focus on security and privacy, yet they are related to a happy, productive life online. I encourage you to read up on them as more research is published. If anything, I feel like this all points to the broader note we touch upon throughout this book: balance your online activity with ample time away from screens. And remember, the online and offline worlds don't always have to be at odds with each other. Want to binge-watch a couple of sitcoms? Take your tablet to the gym and prop it up on the treadmill. Look at that—you're enjoying the digital world and getting off your duff and working off your morning bear claw at the same time! Again, balance. Look for opportunities to strike one for your child and yourself.

When to Get a Smartphone

Now, let's get down to some real nitty-gritty: what's the right age to get your kid their first smartphone?

This is a question I get asked all the time. Guess what? There's no set answer. Everyone has their own. This expert, that expert, you, your kid, everyone has their idea about the "right" age. But everyone should agree that there are lots of angles to be considered: Is your kid responsible enough to take care of it? What does your kid want to do with it? Do they want one to "keep up" with other friends who have one? Is your kid prepared for *a whole new world* that will open up to them via apps, social media, geotracking, texting, ecommerce, online gaming, and on and on and on?

The truth about cell phone ownership is that we're actually talking about giving an adult device to a teen. It's much like when they first get their driver's license and want the keys to borrow the car. A new world of power, mobility, and independence opens up to them when they "get the keys" to their first smartphone.

---

[39] https://www.inc.com/christina-desmarais/science-says-facebook-can-be-terrible-for-your-mental-health-6-great-apps-to-use-instead.html

Immediately we can take that comparison a step further: you get a lot of training before you get your license to drive. Maybe we should think about some training before they get their first phone. At the very least, hopefully they've already been the beneficiary of advice and guidance for online life like I've outlined in previous chapters. But let's get a bit more specific for this age group.

Before they get their first smartphone, I recommend that you ease them into some of the more "advanced" aspects of the digital world via a tablet or your home computer where you can monitor their activity. For example, perhaps your tween or teen wants to share photos on Instagram. They don't *absolutely* need a phone for that. They can just as easily open an account via a tablet or computer and participate from there—although they won't be able to immediately take and share photos like they could from a phone. Which is a good thing! That gives them time to pause and ponder if they should post what they want to post, and maybe even gives you a moment to review what they plan to share online. (See chapter 2 for a review of the guidelines I set forth there.)

Further, you should have them share their username and password with you so that you can monitor their usage and activity. Absolutely do this, at least in the beginning, and absolutely let your kid know that you're doing it. Set conditions for how long you'll do so, and keep the communication going as you monitor their use and see them mature into a good user such that you can cut the apron-strings and let them manage their own account. This goes for social media accounts, email accounts, games they play, or any other account your kid wants to sign up for. Not only are you in charge, you're also responsible for them. Going this route in the early stages of their semi-independent internet usage will allow you to encourage good habits, spot problems, *resolve* problems, and ultimately build trust, all while protecting your kid.

OK, so there's no guarantee that a kid won't choose to get around this by simply creating a second account on their own where they get into all sorts of trouble and mischief. It's been known to happen, particularly because this is the age when children start to tug at how tethered they are. They will start to hide apps used to communicate with friends and the like. The idea here, however, is to mitigate such behavior by setting expectations early and then easing restrictions over time. You do have more direct options available if you find yourself needing them, like the parental control software I mentioned in chapter 2. Many have features that provide alerts when someone attempts to access "blocked" content, when apps are downloaded, and how much time is being spent on certain devices and apps. Some families will want to take that approach. Just know that it's important to use dialogue in conjunction with such features: they won't work as a replacement for parental attention—they're simply tools to make your presence and guidance stronger and more effective.

Another intermediary step you can take is to go *old school* and give your kid a flip phone. Yes, you can still get a flip phone or equivalent. This way, you still give your kid the ability to communicate by voice and through some basic texting functionality without the worry of opening up the entire internet to them. It also gets them in the habit of caring for, and keeping track of, a personal device. (Believe me, it will take them a little bit of practice. Count on it getting misplaced or left behind somewhere at least once, if not more. My kids had the habit of leaving their phones on top of cars, and you can guess the outcome.) Similarly, if your kid wants a smartphone for listening to tunes, there's a way around that too. Hop online and scan your local classifieds for an old iPod or MP3 music player. They can load up their songs and be on their way, again without needing to hop on the internet with a smartphone to do it.

These intermediary steps circle back to the earlier questions about why your kid wants a smartphone. You may find that the answers are relatively simple at first and that a smartphone would be overkill in terms of cost and the risks involved. It's encouraging to know you can get your teen into a smartphone in stages rather than in one universe-expanding fell swoop where the internet rushes in and you find you and your teen are completely overwhelmed.

So, let's say you've gone through this "training period" of sorts with your young teen, or you're starting to feel that a first smartphone might make sense. Pause. Remember, you're the boss here. You get to make a value judgment as to whether or not your kid is ready. If you're overseeing their internet usage (and even participating in it with them to some degree, like I outlined in chapter 2), you'll have a fine sense of what "ready" looks like. When you feel the time is approaching to approve that purchase, I suggest you consider a few more criteria:

- How's your kid been doing with screen time? Do you have a hard time pulling them away from a screen when you say it's time? If that's happening, they may not be ready for the mobile and persistent internet a smartphone provides.
- See which of your kid's friends have a smartphone. If you know their parents, talk to them about their experience and their decision. Some helpful advice from your peer group can go a long way.
- Get a set of rules ready. (You're the boss, remember? And you're likely paying for this!) Be clear about what they are:
  o Will you have access to their social media accounts? Or will you even allow them to have social media accounts on their phone at all? (No need to start off with those right away. They can grow into them over time when you feel they're ready.)
  o Will you activate location sharing so you can track where your kid is?
  o What are the rules for buying things online, like in-app purchases on games?
  o And, critically, what will be the guidelines for sharing *any* kind of personal information about themselves and the family? Set all of these down— in writing is best. Keep in mind that these rules and guidelines will evolve and change.
- Along those lines, take a look at some contracts posted online. These are pledges taken by both parents and kids to promote safe and good times online. Common Sense Media[40] has one, as does ConnectSafely.org.[41] Even if you don't choose to actually put a contract to pen and paper, they offer plenty of food for thought as you set expectations and rules for smartphone use.

---

[40] https://www.commonsensemedia.org/research/technology-addiction-concern-controversy-and-finding-balance/resources
[41] https://www.connectsafely.org/family-contract-smartphone-use

- Extend the same parental controls to their smartphone and see if your smartphone includes screen time and app limits features as part of the operating system, like the ones Apple introduced with their iOS 12. Together, these will allow you to keep an eye on usage and give you the means to loosen those controls as your teen gets older and more responsible. Plus, apps and features like these help you manage how much data your teen is dumping into their data lake. There's no need to open those data floodgates right away! Limit their usage, and thus their data creation. In addition, most mobile operators offer you the ability to monitor and manage data consumption. There are even apps that will throttle certain data-hungry apps and turn those apps off if you approach your data threshold.

I'll wrap up the conversation with a concise yet striking data point: according to Nielsen research posted in 2017, about 45% of U.S. children aged 10 to 12 have a smartphone with a data service plan that allows them to access the internet.[42] What's the driver behind that? Parents said it was because they wanted to get a hold of their kid easily. But take a look at the most popular responses that immediately follow:

---

[42] https://www.nielsen.com/us/en/insights/news/2017/mobile-kids--the-parent-the-child-and-the-smartphone.html

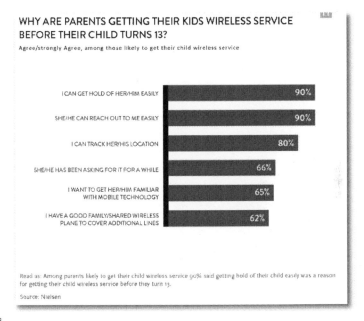

WHY ARE PARENTS GETTING THEIR KIDS WIRELESS SERVICE BEFORE THEIR CHILD TURNS 13?

Agree/strongly Agree, among those likely to get their child wireless service

I CAN GET HOLD OF HER/HIM EASILY	90%
SHE/HE CAN REACH OUT TO ME EASILY	90%
I CAN TRACK HER/HIS LOCATION	80%
SHE/HE HAS BEEN ASKING FOR IT FOR A WHILE	66%
I WANT TO GET HER/HIM FAMILIAR WITH MOBILE TECHNOLOGY	65%
I HAVE A GOOD FAMILY/SHARED WIRELESS PLANE TO COVER ADDITIONAL LINES	62%

Read as: Among parents likely to get their child wireless service 90% said getting hold of their child easily was a reason for getting their child wireless service before they turn 13.

Source: Nielsen

43

Outside of "I can track her/his location," you can do much of the above simply by giving your kid a starter phone without an internet connection, as I explained above. And as for the "She/he has been asking for it a while," remember, you're the boss. You'll know when they're *really* ready and you're ready to start them on their journey. Just be sure to give them the opportunity to prove it. Take an active role and lead the way.

Creating a Smartphone Contract with Your Kid

Something you should consider while teaching your tween or teen social responsibility and good smartphone etiquette is to introduce a smartphone contract. This should not be an onerous, legalese multi-page tome but rather a simple set of rules that you *both* agree to abide by and that is tuned to your specific family beliefs. Like other topics in this book, you should discuss this and seek agreement with your tween or teen so they have a vested interest in

---

[43] Ibid.

adhering to what's agreed to before committing pen to paper. You should also be willing to modify the contract as circumstances warrant. There are lots of sample contracts posted online. One that I find meets the needs of most parents is available on the Verywell Family website:

This contract between [Parents' Names Go Here] and [Child's Name Goes Here] seeks to establish family rules and consequences regarding cell phone usage.

Son or Daughter Cell Phone Responsibilities

- *I will not send threatening or mean texts to others*
- *I will not text or place phone calls after 9 p.m.*
- *I will keep my phone charged at all times*
- *I will not bring my cell phone to the family dinner table*
- *I will not go over our plan's monthly minutes or text message limits. If I do, I understand that I may be responsible for paying any additional charges or that I may lose my cell phone privileges*
- *I understand that I am responsible for knowing where my phone is, and for keeping it in good condition*
- *I understand that my cell phone may be taken away if I talk back to my parents, I fail to do my chores, or I fail to keep my grades up*
- *I will obey rules of etiquette regarding cell phones in public places. I will make sure my phone is turned off when I am in church, in restaurants, or quiet settings*
- *I will obey any rules my school has regarding cell phones, such as turning them off during class, or keeping them on vibrate while riding the school bus*
- *I promise I will alert my parents when I receive suspicious or alarming phone calls or text messages from people I don't know*
- *I will also alert my parents if I am being harassed by someone via my cell phone*
- *I will not use my cell phone to bully another*
- *I will send no more than _____ texts per day*
- *I understand that having a cell phone can be helpful in an emergency, but I know that I must still practice good*

judgment and make good choices that will keep me out of trouble or out of danger

- *I will not send embarrassing photos of my family or friends to others. In addition, I will not use my phone's camera to take embarrassing photos of others*

- *I understand that having a cell phone is a privilege and that if I fail to adhere to this contract, my cell phone privilege may be revoked*

- *If needed, I may help pay for the cost of the phone and/or for excess charges that I incur without permission from my parents*

Cell Phone Contract Parent Responsibilities

- *I understand that I will make myself available to answer any questions my tween might have about owning a cell phone and using it responsibly*

- *I will support my child when he or she alerts me to an alarming message or text message that he or she has received*

- *I will alert my child if our cell phone plan changes and impacts the plan's minutes*

- *I will give my child _____ warning(s) before I take his or her cell phone away*

Signed _____ *(Son or Daughter)*
Signed _____ *(Parents)*
Date _____ [44]

Cyberbullies (Part Two)

We talked about cyberbullying in detail in chapter 2, yet it's such a prevalent problem that it begs revisiting it now that we're talking about tweens and teens.

The first thing I want to get across is that cyberbullying happens. And it happens way too often.

---

[44] https://www.verywellfamily.com/a-sample-cell-phone-contract-for-parents-and-tweens-3288540

According to research published in 2016 from the Cyberbullying Research Center, through a survey of 5,700 kids ages 12 to 17 in U.S. middle schools and high schools, 36.7% of girls and 30.5% of boys reported that they have experienced some form of cyberbullying in their lifetime. Girls were more likely to say that it took the form of others spreading rumors about them online, while boys attributed their instances of cyberbullying to threats of harm.[45] Perhaps a bit chilling is that almost 12% of the respondents overall self-reported themselves of having committed an act of cyberbullying in their lifetime.[46]

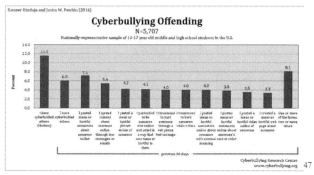

To reiterate the characteristics of cyberbullying, let's look at how StopBullying.gov defines the problem:

Cyberbullying is bullying that takes place over digital devices like cell phones, computers, and tablets. Cyberbullying can occur through SMS, Text, and apps, or online in social media, forums, or gaming where people can view, participate in, or share content. Cyberbullying includes sending, posting, or sharing negative, harmful, false, or mean content about someone else. It can include sharing personal or private information about someone else causing embarrassment or humiliation. Some cyberbullying crosses the line into unlawful or criminal behavior.[48]

Clearly, there are plenty of ways we can hurt others online. And cyberbullying certainly differs versus its pre-cyber variety, which

---

[45] https://cyberbullying.org/2016-cyberbullying-data
[46] Ibid.
[47] Ibid.
[48] https://www.stopbullying.gov/cyberbullying/what-is-it/index.html

took place face-to-face where hurtful comments and threats were flung in person, or rumors were shared in conversations or via notes passed in class. Proximity mattered and reach was limited. Today, it's anonymous and public. A cyberbully can hide behind a screen and say what they want without being identified. Hurtful notes are now social media entries and posts on forums where practically anyone can see them. And it's permanent. As with all things posted online, it leaves a record that lasts—even if a post is taken down, there's no guarantee that someone hasn't grabbed a screenshot of it, which allows the hurt to live on and potentially haunt both the victim and bully as colleges and employers conduct reputation searches on them later in life.

Cyberbullying is no joke. It has both immediate and lasting impacts. Many victims report that they experience:

- *Depression and anxiety, increased feelings of sadness and loneliness, changes in sleep and eating patterns, and loss of interest in activities they used to enjoy. These issues may persist into adulthood.*
- *Health complaints.*
- *Decreased academic achievement—GPA and standardized test scores—and school participation. They are more likely to miss, skip, or drop out of school.*[49]

And many kids who are cyberbullies show a greater inclination to:

- *Abuse alcohol and other drugs in adolescence and as adults.*
- *Get into fights, vandalize property, and drop out of school.*
- *Engage in early sexual activity.*
- *Have criminal convictions and traffic citations as adults.*
- *Be abusive toward their romantic partners, spouses, or children as adults.*[50]

Just as discussed in chapter 2, it may not be readily apparent to you if your child is a victim of cyberbullying. After all, you're not

---

[49] https://www.stopbullying.gov/at-risk/effects/index.html
[50] Ibid.

constantly looking over his or her shoulder. It could be only one text or one post, and something you'd probably miss, but it could hit your kid like a bull's-eye arrow shot. This is important enough to reiterate what I shared in chapter 2 about behavioral indicators of cyberbullying you need to be aware of. These include if your child:

- *Suddenly stops using the computer, even though [he or she has] always enjoyed it before.*
- *Doesn't want to use the computer in a place where you can see it.*
- *Turns off the computer monitor, or changes screens every time you walk by.*
- *Seems nervous or jumpy when he gets an instant message, text, or email.*
- *Alludes to bullying indirectly by saying something like "there's a lot of drama at school," or "I have no friends."*
- *Doesn't want to go to school or appears uneasy about going.*
- *Becomes withdrawn.*[51]

Any of these signs are your cue to get involved and find out what's really going on, and that begins with a conversation. Be aware that this conversation may not be with you, and that's all right. Some children may find it easier to bring it up to another relative or a close family friend instead of bringing it forward to their parents or guardians. Again, this is all right. The important thing is to get them talking about it, at least for starters. After that, you can step in. You may feel angry, upset, and maybe even helpless. Take a deep breath and roll up your sleeves because there is plenty you can do.

Do not respond with messages or posts of your own. You may want to strike back. Absolutely do not. You may feel that you should fight fire with fire. This will result in doing more harm than good.

Instead, get to work. Start documenting everything. Get screenshots of the offending texts or activity. Capture the

---

[51] https://www.understood.org/en/friends-feelings/child-social-situations/online-activities-social-media/how-to-tell-if-your-child-is-being-bullied-online

screenname of the person posting it, time, date—think and act like a detective gathering evidence. Use this when you make reports.

Report it. Cyberbullying almost always violates the terms of service on websites, social media platforms, and other internet services. Many of these services have mechanisms to report negative posts, which can get them removed. Make use of them. Get that content off the internet and alert the service to the person who is responsible.

Monitor it closely. If you get the post removed the cyberbully may look for other ways to keep affecting your child.

Break off contact with the offender(s). Go into your social media settings for the services you are using and block offending users. Tighten down the privacy settings that control who can see your child's posts and who can contact them. You may even want to consider getting them off the social media platform until you can sort things out. It's common for people to take a break from social media when it appears that things have spiraled out of control. Your kid may push back, but this may be your best option.

Determine if it breaks the law. This is an important distinction to make. Plenty of cyberbullying falls into the category of mean, hurtful remarks that are said in the heat of the moment or are the result of a feud. They're to be taken seriously, of course. Yet, some cyberbullying crosses the line into illegal activity, such as threats of violence, sexually explicit photos, Peeping Tom pictures of people in private situations (like changing rooms or shots into your home through the window), and stalking (more on that in a moment). If you're *at all* concerned that you have a case of this, contact your local law enforcement for guidance. They'll show you the way.

Tell the school about it. Even if the perpetrator is anonymous, let the school know what is happening to your child. Chances are, your school district or even your state has codes and policies in place that cover not only bullying in school but cyberbullying outside of school as well. Get in touch with a counselor or administrator at your school and see what support and recourse you have available to you.

Finally, support your child. To some degree or other, they have been hurt, even if they don't let on about it or they attempt to brush it off. There's no one answer here because cyberbullying takes on such varying forms and degrees and it impacts people differently. However, take a look at the circumstances and determine if you and your family need additional support, whether from a counselor at school, a leader at your church, mosque, or synagogue, or even a mental health professional. As said earlier, bullying of any kind can leave permanent marks that damage a person's well-being and confidence for years to come. Address it now. Don't let it fester.

To that point, what if you hear about or witness another child being cyberbullied? This can be tricky because what you interpret as cyberbullying may be someone else's idea of good-natured bantering. I'm not suggesting you brush it off. In this case, reflecting on the steps above, you will have to use your best judgment on how to proceed. For example, if you think one of your child's friends has been impacted, ask your kid if they think their friend was offended by whatever was posted.

Worse yet, what if you suspect that your child is taking part in cyberbullying? I can't imagine a more disheartening reality than realizing that one of my children knowingly cyberbullied someone. I would feel like I failed as a parent and digital citizen. If you think your child has either cyberbullied someone themselves or piled on to a cyberbullying incident, you should sit them down and explain that you will not, under any circumstances, tolerate this type of behavior—and that if it continues they will not only lose access to all their devices but will also face more severe forms of punishment as you see fit to curb this behavior. In this case your tone should reflect the severity of what they've done. This is a time to be firm and decisive.

You may be wondering why I've devoted so much of this book to this topic. There are primarily two reasons. First, the trauma from cyberbullying can result in a lifetime of issues for those affected. The thought of this activity stifling a bright future should make all of us pause.

Researching bullying and cyberbullying among adolescents, Rosario Ortega found that victims suffer psychosocial problems like depression, social anxiety, and low self-esteem. She points out that 93% of the victims experienced upset, embarrassment, anger, frustration, vulnerability, fear, sadness, defenselessness, hopelessness, depression, and anxiety. Cybervictimization can also cause affective disorders and a greater chance of internalizing adjustment problems. Over time, persistent cyberbullying can lead to sustained mental illness.[52]

Second, in severe instances, those affected take their own lives. The link between cyberbullying and suicide has been the subject of research for some time. According to Benjamin Shain, MD, PhD, the lead author of an American Academy of Pediatrics study, "Bullying has always been a major issue for adolescents, but there is now greater recognition of the connection between bullying and suicide," Shain explains.[53] And he goes on to state that cyberbullying is "as serious a problem as face-to-face bullying." It's understandable to want to view cyberbullying as somehow less harmful because it happens online, but with Shain's statements in mind, the results from a survey given to nearly 2,000 middle school children back in 2007 are particularly chilling: "Youth who experienced traditional bullying or cyberbullying, as either an offender or a victim, had more suicidal thoughts and were more likely to attempt suicide than those who had not experienced such forms of peer aggression."[54] Literature from the U.S. Centers for Disease Control and Prevention directs school personnel on the topic accordingly: "Provide support and referrals for all youth involved. Include their families."[55] The literature goes on to say that instances of cyberbullying require punishment and consequences for the perpetrators, yet professional mental health support is vital for all parties involved if communities,

---

[52] https://www.usrepresented.com/2016/12/10/the-long-term-effects-of-cyberbullying/
[53] https://www.aap.org/en-us/about-the-aap/aap-press-room/Pages/With-suicide-Now-Teens%E2%80%99-Second-Leading-Cause-of-Death-Pediatricians-Urged-to-Ask-About-its-Risks.aspx
[54] https://www.ncbi.nlm.nih.gov/pubmed/20658375/
[55] https://www.cdc.gov/violenceprevention/pdf/bullying-suicide-translation-final-a.pdf

schools, and families are to quash the source of cyberbullying and prevent future suffering.

Cyberstalking

Another issue that can arise at this age is cyberstalking. While related to cyberbullying in some ways, it stands on its own as a unique issue. In an article published by the Cyberbullying Research Center, Sameer Hinduja cites several sources in defining cyberstalking as:

Involving the use of technology (most often, the Internet!) to make someone else afraid or concerned about their safety. Generally speaking, this conduct is threatening or otherwise fear-inducing, involves an invasion of a person's relative right to privacy, and manifests in repeated actions over time. Most of the time, those who cyberstalk use social media, Internet databases, search engines, and other online resources to intimidate, follow, and cause anxiety or terror to others.

Surprisingly, cyberstalking rarely occurs by a stranger (although we do hear about those cases when they involve celebrities and rabid fans), and most often is carried out by a person the target knows intimately or professionally. For example, the aggressor may be an ex-girlfriend or ex-boyfriend, former friend, past employee, or an acquaintance who wants to control, possess, scare, threaten, or actually harm the other person. In many cases, they have had access to certain personal information, accounts, inboxes, or other private knowledge regarding their target's daily routine, lifestyle, or life choices.[56]

Although most instances of cyberstalking involve someone known by the victim, that is not always the case. Consider what happened to Nisha,[57] as reported in an article on The Quint website:

Nisha, a journalist from Lucknow, received a call from an unknown number at 11:05 pm. Truecaller displayed 'Aryan Matina' as the caller.

Since she did not know who the caller was, she decided not to pick up. Almost instantly, she got a notification on her Facebook profile: a friend request from a guy named, 'Aryan Matina'.

---

[56] https://cyberbullying.org/cyberstalking
[57] Nisha's name has been changed to protect her identity.

Without much ado, she blocked him on Facebook and his number on her phone. Within a few minutes she got another call from an unknown number. The same name flashed on Truecaller. She blocked it yet again.

This, however, was not going to be a one-off incident. It was just the beginning of repeated cyberstalking that is still ongoing.

Minutes after the message, he sent her a photograph, which had her face and her phone number on it and said, 'ready for sex'. He threatened her further. He said that if she didn't unblock him, he would post this picture on social media.[58]

The article goes on to reflect the horror Nisha faced trying to shake her cyberstalker. Nisha felt the only way to combat her cyberstalker was to go public with her ordeal, which then led her cyberstalker to claim he was so distraught that he was going to take his own life.

The steps for addressing a cyberstalker situation are very similar to cyberbullying. The one distinction is how quickly you bring it to law enforcement's attention. A cyberstalker may follow their victim into the everyday world and become a stalker who follows a child home, to school, or elsewhere. Note that this has become increasingly easy to do, as there are apps that include location services that allow users to share where they are at any given time or if they are in the vicinity of each other. This is particularly important to keep in mind because stalkers are often someone the victim knows, which only increases the risk to children because the stalker takes advantage of familiarity and trust. In addition, notify the social media platform of the cybercrime. Be sure to keep records of what happened, including screen shots, URLs, and any other information that may help identify the cyberstalker. In particular, be sure to reach out to the grievance officer of the social media platform(s) and explain to them what is happening as well.

These past two sections may have been difficult for you to read. It's a tough topic, as we don't like to even imagine such a thing happening to our kids. But, like many tough topics, it's a necessary

---

[58] https://www.thequint.com/neon/gender/stalker-threatens-woman-journalist-cyberstalking#gs.QKkLg7OY

one to discuss in an unflinching way. What's tougher yet is if any of this happens to your family. I've met my share of children, parents, and people who are now adults who have experienced cyberbullying and cyberstalking. The pain and damage they've suffered are quite real. That's why I can't stress it enough—if you suspect cyberbullying or cyberstalking is taking place, you must act and act quickly.

Making Online Friends and Friendships

A friend of mine has a teenage son who's pretty typical in that he likes to pop on the headset and catch up with his buddies by playing games on his Xbox video game console: "Dad, I'm gonna hit the servers and see what my peeps are up to online." Those friends are a mix of kids he knows personally from school and his sports teams, and perhaps even a few kids he's met at summer camp over the years. It's a little cross-section of his social life, and it's almost like a big dinner party where friends of friends meet and become friends themselves. Also in that mix are people his son has never met in person before. They'll have met through a game online, and somehow or other they'll strike up a conversation that goes beyond, "Hey, nice shot." So, it's something that actually turns into an online friendship.

It so happened that my friend's son pulled him aside one day, a little concerned. His son, being up on the news, knew that a natural disaster had struck the place where his online friend lived. His pal hadn't been online for days, and, honestly, he was worried. They'd never exchanged email addresses or phone numbers (as my friend told his son never to share that kind of personal information online, even with a friend like this), so there was no way for him to know if his friend was all right. They talked about it for a bit, with my friend acknowledging and supporting his son's concern. Then they hoped for the best.

Turns out, a week later, his friend was back online. Both he and his family were safe, and all was well enough in their world that it was time to play on the Xbox again.

This represents something new for today's parents—your kids are likely to develop friendships with people they've never met in person and probably never will. This happens quite a bit in the world of online gaming, where chat channels and voice channels are built right into the gaming experience. Friendships of this stripe are a "new normal" of sorts, and they're not limited to online gaming.

It may be hard for those of us who didn't grow up in this kind of environment, but it's important to recognize that some of these "digital" friendships are just as real to your kids as the ones they make at school, through sports, in activities, at your place of worship, and so forth. We should recognize them as such and not diminish them simply because they've never met face-to-face. In fact, it's likely that some of us also have working relationships and friendships with folks we've never met in person.

It's very much the new normal, but that certainly doesn't mean it's risk-free for kids or adults to just go out and start creating online friendships. Yet, there's an important difference for kids because online friendships have become so common: If you have an online relationship with a co-worker or business associate, you have a pretty firm idea of who they are. Namely, that they are who they say they are! And that's definitely not the case in the broader online world. Whether you're a kid or an adult, you have to realize that people online are not always who they claim to be, which can lead to serious consequences, such as Alicia's story in chapter 2.

So, what's the advice when it comes to striking up friendships online—whether through games, social media, or anywhere else? First off, you can flip back to the advice I passed along in chapter 2 under the section about "The Talk." That same guidance applies here as well. While you don't want your kid to be afraid of others they meet for the first time online, you absolutely want them to be guarded. In fact, you don't want them sharing *any* kind of personal information like where they live, where they go to school, who they are friends with, when and where they're going on vacation, their phone number, their email, or their full name. You get the idea. Again, not to scare you, but to be absolutely clear about the potential risks, realize that there are people who intentionally target kids—to groom them for illegal activity, sexual encounters, or in the worst cases, with the aim of abducting them. Again, we remind ourselves of Alicia's story.

As with so many topics we've discussed in this book so far, a vital preventive measure is to talk with your kids. Sit in with them and listen in on their chats while they're playing a video game. Ask who they're hanging out with online. None of this should feel like an interrogation. You need to maintain the tone of a normal conversation about their friends and what they're all up to. After all, this is another aspect of their developing social life. Take the same interest in your child's online friends and friendships that you do with the friends they hang out with both in and out of school—and take the extra care to let your kid know the difference between what they can share with friends they know well in the face-to-face world and with people they'll want to consider as friends after meeting them in the digital world.

A great example of the power of having an ongoing dialogue with your children comes from Raj Samani, my good friend and McAfee's Chief Scientist. Raj has three beautiful children. We are very like-minded when it comes to raising kids, and we both believe it's imperative that we regularly talk with our children as they navigate their digital world and build online behaviors. He shared a quick story about his oldest daughter who'd recently changed schools. As she got acquainted with her new schoolmates, she realized that some of the friends from her old school were not only removed by proximity but by divergent interests as well, which is typical for young teens. And on top of that, a relationship had turned sour, which again is sometimes a sad fact of teenage life. Using the diplomacy and online etiquette that her father and mother had taught her, she sent the following to her friend:

"Hi Jane [actual name withheld], this friendship was never based on common things that we both liked, but on proximity—once I left and when we weren't able to see each other nearly every day. Our friendship turned toxic. Don't take this the wrong way—Remember all the amazing moments, but I think it's time to dock the boat. Bye."

Play close attention to the tone. There was balance and reflection rather than bitterness or animosity. She effectively used great communication skills and a messaging app (in this case WhatsApp) to deliver a challenging message for resolving what could have escalated into a difficult situation for herself and her friend had they tried to press on in their current situation. I have no doubt that your child will have friends come and go. Some real and some online. Giving them the tools to navigate these relationships will help reduce the heartache and stress that often accompanies that part of their journey.

The Secret Digital Life of Teens

Fact of life: Tweens and teens hide stuff from their parents. Always have. Always will.

Let's try and think back to when we were teenagers. And we can do so with the perspective parenting or age has given us—and hopefully at least an iota of wisdom. First, we know this is a time of burgeoning independence. They're champing at the bit to establish their own lives, their sense of self, their confidence, and their friendships both online and offline. There's also plenty of body chemistry happening, which manifests in all manner of emotional and physical changes that are further compounded by social pressures and the fact that their brains are still developing—particularly the parts that govern judgment and impulse control. Ah, to be a teen again! (No thanks!)

So, is it really any surprise that many teens have a furtive, or even totally secret, life online?

The numbers bear it out. One online survey of parents and teens found that 44% of teens say they hide their online activity from their parents. What's more, 46% of teens would change their behaviors if they knew their parents were watching.[59] Granted, some of this behavior reflects their desire for privacy, which is understandable for a young person on the road to adulthood. Not every interaction online needs to come up for inspection. Yet the obvious issue is that they're still your kids, teens at that, and they'll push boundaries.

---

[59] https://securingtomorrow.mcafee.com/consumer/family-safety/digital-divide/

They'll visit sites, watch movies, and engage in conversations that you would disapprove of—and likely with good reason because of their age or the rules you've established for your household. So it's no stretch to say that tweens and teens have secret digital lives, at least to some degree.

We've talked a bit about parental controls as a means to address this, yet what also begs a conversation is how these secret lives can take shape via social media. A while back, I came across a great article by Ana Homayoun, a noted author, speaker, and school consultant on the topic of tweens and teens. In it, she states the following:

I've spent nearly two decades working with teens on organization and time-management in the heart of the Silicon Valley, and many teen girls tell me they have a real Instagram account ("rinsta") for a wider audience and then keep a "finsta" (friends-only or "fake" Instagram) for their closest friends. Many teens use shortened versions of their names or aliases for finsta accounts, which they often see as an opportunity to share a less edited, less filtered version of their lives. They might spend a lot of time trying to capture the perfect Instagram photo for the "rinsta," which reaches a wider general audience, while a finsta might reveal, as one high school sophomore girl declared, "my innermost thoughts."[60]

Homayoun goes on to say that the issue with such behaviors can be this:

The ready availability of tools to hide teen social media use can be problematic, leading teens to overshare images, videos and commentary. But that privacy has long been proven to be unreliable, because information shared within a private group can be easily captured in a screenshot and shared with a wider audience. The notion of privacy online is only as reliable as teens' relationships with other users, and that combined with general privacy concerns provides little guarantee that online information will ever be kept secret.[61]

Once more we're presented with the black-and-white truth: the internet is forever. This is an instance where teens may be pumping some muck of their own into the data lake, which future employers

---

[60] https://www.nytimes.com/2017/06/07/well/family/the-secret-social-media-lives-of-teenagers.html
[61] Ibid.

and college admissions boards, not to mention future love interests, may dredge up later in life. Homayoun presents another common-sense conclusion about this behavior as well. Kids (and adults) place value on "likes" in social media as a form of recognition, in her words, "a barometer for popularity," which can lead to creating posts and images that are a cry for immediate "likes" rather than a reflection of their actual values and beliefs. If I can paraphrase it bluntly—kids (and adults) will even do dumb things for "likes," such as eating Tide PODS® or doing the cinnamon challenge.

What to do about this? It's time to reinforce earlier notions that your teen should consider anything he or she posts as part of their permanent record. I don't necessarily think it's wrong to have a couple of Instagram or other accounts—one for a broader set of friends and another for closer friends. What matters is how those accounts are used and, of course, what your teen is posting on them. This gets back to the importance of that ongoing dialogue with your teen that you started during the formative years.

The Secret Digital Language of Teens

Another sort of secret your teens may keep is their own digital language. Well, maybe this isn't so much a *secret* because you may have seen some of this language on their smartphone from time to time when a chat notification pops up; still, it can certainly feel that way when you see a message that you absolutely can't read. Like, "123 BRB." Not without a dictionary. (By the way, "123 BRB" translates to "I agree. [123] Be right back. [BRB]"[62])

Some of these little abbreviations are pretty innocuous and just meant to speed up typing in a text. Others indeed are meant to keep you off track of behaviors and activities that, as a parent, you'll definitely want to know about. Here are just a few examples compiled by McAfee's family safety evangelist Toni Birdsong:

- Dime = Attractive person (a perfect 10)
- WUD = What are you doing?
- OBS = Obviously

---

[62] https://www.commonsense.org/education/digital-glossary

- TBH = To be honest (followed by a blunt comment)
- 1174 = Place to meet for a party
- LMIRL = Let's meet in real life[63]

You can find other more comprehensive lists of internet slang quite readily with a search. One example is maintained by Wiktionary, a free online dictionary that, like its sister project the free online encyclopedia Wikipedia, is run by the Wikimedia Foundation.[64] Another is a list of digital slang (and other digital terms in general) that's maintained by Common Sense Media.[65] Verywell Family has a fine article on the topic, as well a list.[66] It's a good idea to keep up on digital slang words because, like any slang, they're likely to change—and they aren't universal by any stretch of the imagination. There's a good chance, in fact, that your tween or teen has never seen or used these terms but has a few of their own that you'll never see on any of these lists. That's the nature of a secret language, after all. Just be aware that your kids are using some form of one, whether it's a matter of convenience or to hide their tracks.

Sexting

As if we don't have enough to deal with when raging hormones, the first driver's license, proms, after-graduation plans, and the swirl of social pressures are all vying for our teen's attention, there's the growing trend of sexting (sending, receiving, or forwarding sexually explicit messages, photographs, or images, primarily between mobile phones, of oneself to others[67]). Sexting has been gaining popularity since around 2010. There are frequent news stories about politicians, celebrities, or well-known business people engaging in sexting. However, it is most common among teens, and there's much you need to know about it. The Verywell Family website offers solid information about sexting and other topics of interest to parents.

---

[63] https://securingtomorrow.mcafee.com/consumer/family-safety/2018-texting-slang-update-decode-teen-saying-online/
[64] https://en.wiktionary.org/wiki/Appendix:English_internet_slang
[65] https://www.commonsense.org/education/digital-glossary
[66] https://www.verywellfamily.com/a-teen-slang-dictionary-2610994
[67] https://en.wikipedia.org/wiki/Sexting

First off, teen sexting is child pornography. Laws vary, yet some states in the U.S. consider the exchange of nude photos of minors as a felony offense, even if the exchange is consensual. Additionally, some states can label a teen as a sex offender for sending or possessing such photos, even if the photos are of them. It almost goes without saying that some research shows a majority of teens don't know sexting is a form of child pornography in the eyes of the law. It's critical to convey to your teen exactly what it is and the accordingly harsh penalties for it.

Above and beyond the law, sexting can expose teens to tremendous danger in the form of sexual bullying meant to embarrass and humiliate the victim; sexual predators who may exploit such photos if they go public on the internet; and the age-old practice of blackmail, where the threat of sharing the photos can put the victim in thrall to the person who holds them.

Last, like anything else we share via the internet (whether we believe we are sharing it privately or not), sexts never go away—they can go public and stay public for good. Likewise, the reputational harm that follows lasts forever as well.[68]

If you think your child is already engaging in sexting, a tempered response with a balanced and moderate tone will most likely get the best results: using a heavy hand will increase the risk of them tuning you out and defiantly continuing the behavior. Again, Verywell Family offers parents great suggestions:

> *The best approach to talking about sexting is to take a non-judgmental and informational one. Keeping the dialogue open leaves room for your kids to talk with you rather than hiding things away. Also, be aware that kids may have a different name for sexting, so you'll need to be clear about the topic you are discussing. Try some simple conversation starters to break the ice:*

- *"Have you heard about this sexting thing? Do you know anything about it?"*

---

[68] https://www.verywellfamily.com/things-teens-do-not-know-about-sexting-but-should-460654

- *"I was watching TV/reading the news the other day and saw a story about some kids who got in trouble for sending [use your own word here—suggestive, sexy, naked, etc.] pictures to friends. Did you hear about that?"*
- *"Can we talk about the types of things you and your friends like to share online? I want to make sure you're taking care of yourself and looking out for your friends, as well."*

Rather than leading the conversation, make sure you listen to your tween/teen. Your child may not agree with you about what is and isn't appropriate and may have some compelling reasons why. Encourage your child to think about the possible consequences and how your child wants to be seen by others.[69]

One healthy option is to broach the issue before they take a turn at sexting—as soon as your child has access to a smartphone or a webcam. This may feel awkward to you as you're sure your child would never indulge in such an activity. However, since you've committed to having an ongoing dialogue with your child as part of your desire to continuously inform and educate them on how to be safe online, this will just be another topic along that continuum.

Black Hats – Exposure to Hackers and Hacking through Gaming

Hey look, the subject of gaming has come up again! That's because it offers plenty to talk about. In this case, it gives us a clear-cut example of how pervasive and accessible the basic tools for cybercrime have become.

In 2017, the UK's National Crime Agency (NCA) published an intelligence assessment report that came with a warning: off-the-shelf hacking tools that require little to no technical expertise are becoming available to gamers online.[70] In fact, YouTube is full of instructional videos for those who want to venture down this path. Why would gamers, in particular, use these tools? There are a few

---

[69] https://www.verywellfamily.com/what-is-sexting-problem-1258921
[70] https://nationalcrimeagency.gov.uk/who-we-are/publications/6-pathways-into-cyber-crime-1/file

reasons. Some are used to create cheats that give a player an advantage in an online game. Others are used to attack the network other players are using to access the online game—known as Denial of Service (DoS) or Distributed Denial of Service (DDoS) attacks—by flooding the other player's network with useless requests at such a rate that it makes the home network unusable for, usually, a limited stretch of time. This is referred to as "booting," and in many cases this is a child's first encounter with conducting a cybercrime. What the report also found, via interviews of the young culprits who used them, was that they didn't think any of these activities were illegal:

Indeed, one member of a hacking collective which sold DDoS tools and botnet services told police that a warning from law enforcement would have made him stop.[71]

These sometimes unknowing, unwitting, and unskilled perpetrators of cybercrime are as young as 13 and 14 years old and are sometimes referred to as "skiddies" or "script kiddies." It's not to say that these children go on to lives as fully fledged cybercrooks, yet the NCA does note, "the proliferation of off-the-shelf hacking tools and services has brought the ability to cause significant harm within reach of the young and relatively unskilled cybercriminals."

This tells us a few things. First, it's utterly essential to have a full suite of security products protecting your home network and the devices on them, and to even consider a home network security device that protects your home at the source—your Wi-Fi router (see chapter 1). The reason is simple—hacking has become a commodity. People can order it up like a pizza. It's also provided as a service for those who don't want to get bogged down in the technical details.

Second, talk to your kids about cybercrime in general. To hack apps and software is to break the user agreement they come with and, in some cases, is illegal. Obviously, paying someone, anyone, to boot a player off a game and render their home network unusable with a DoS or DDoS attack is flat-out illegal. If they see any of this

---

activity, they should steer clear of it. Likewise, if a certain player is making threats or claims of a hack or attack, many gaming platforms allow you to report the user for such behavior. Let them know they can use that avenue as well.

On its Xbox Support pages, Microsoft offers a concise, plain-spoken article with answers to frequently asked questions about what these attacks look like and what you can do about them. Some of their advice includes:

- *Reset your Internet router.*
- *Contact your ISP.*
- *If you are certain of the identity of the DoS or DDoS attacker:*
- *Contact the attacker's ISP.*
- *File a complaint against the player with Xbox Live. Select the "tampering" category on the complaint form.*
- *Avoid that individual on Xbox Live in the future.*[72]

Behavior Plays a Role in Cybercrime Too

Who's low on self-control? Teenagers. OK, OK—not *all* teenagers. And maybe not yours. But it's widely recognized that teens can be a bit more impulsive than the rest of us. Research published in the *Social Science Computer Review* seems to indicate that this impulsivity could make some of them more likely to be victims of cybercrime. But, of course, this can also apply to many adults. Tomas Holt, professor of criminal justice at Michigan State University and lead author of the research, states, "An individual's characteristics are critical in studying how cybercrime perseveres, particularly the person's impulsiveness and the activities that they engage in while online that have the greatest impact on their risk."[73]

I'm well aware that one of major ways this manifested is by clicking on "bad" links to sites that contain malware or viruses—and

---

[72] https://support.xbox.com/en-US/xbox-one/networking/dos-attacks-faq

[73] https://www.futurity.org/cybercrime-security-personality-1935732/

this can happen to the best of us. We may search on a topic, say, a celebrity, and then click on one of the top links in that search. Because hackers know people are constantly doing searches on celebrities, they use them to bait people into visiting malicious sites. My team and I conduct research on this, celebrities in particular, to find out which pop culture icons are being used as bait by hackers. (If you're curious, my 2018 list included Ruby Rose, Kristin Cavallari, and Marion Cotillard in the top three.)[74]

So, if you're wanting to see that clip of Ruby Rose as the new Batwoman, slow down. Be careful of what you click and only visit reputable websites—you know, maybe *The Hollywood Reporter* or *Entertainment Tonight*. Also, security software will often provide you with browsing protection that identifies bad links before they are even clicked. For example, you may see a little red stop sign next to a sketchy web search result. These are two good ways to keep any kind of impulse control in check.

While we are on the topic, we can also talk about phishing attacks. They prey on people's behavior too—namely, the sense of trust we sometimes give out too freely. The dictionary definition of phishing according to Merriam-Webster is, "A scam by which an Internet user is duped (as by a deceptive e-mail message) into revealing personal or confidential information which the scammer can use illicitly." Note the use of the term "duped." Ouch! But that's how it has worked and continues to work. It can take shape like this, as reported by Threatpost in November 2018:

A phishing campaign with a clever Spotify lure has been spotted trying to harvest user credentials for the popular streaming service.

Researchers at AppRiver detected the offensive earlier this month, in a campaign looking to compromise Spotify customers using bogus – but convincing – emails with the purpose of hijacking the owner's account. The emails attempt to dupe users into clicking on a phishing link that would redirect them to a deceptive website. Once at the site, users were prompted to enter their user name

---

[74] https://securingtomorrow.mcafee.com/consumer/consumer-threat-notices/most-dangerous-celebrities-2018/

and password, where it would go directly into the bad guys' repository of compromised things.

Obviously, the credentials could be useful if the victim has reused them on other, higher-value sites, like online banking. However, beyond selling the credentials on the Dark Web, "knowing just one password for a victim opens the door to a multitude of attack vectors," David Pickett, cybersecurity analyst at AppRiver, told Threatpost.[75]

What's most noteworthy about today's breed of phishing attacks is just how credible the fraudsters can make the notification email or communication look. If you blind your critical eye even just a shade or two, the whole thing will look legitimate. Again, impulse control. If one of these emails gets sent to you or your kid—pause and do the following:

- Look out for phishing red flags. If you notice that the "from" address in an email is a little sketchy or an unknown source, don't interact with the message. And if you're still unsure of whether the email is legitimate or not, hover your mouse over the button prompting you to click on the link (but don't actually click on it). If the URL preview doesn't seem to be related to the company, it is most likely a phishing email.
- Be skeptical of emails claiming to come from legitimate companies. If you receive an email asking to confirm your login credentials, go directly to the company's website. You should be able to check the status of your account on the company website or under the settings portion of the app in question to determine the legitimacy of the request.

So, when it comes to hackers, a good defense is to instill in your kids and yourself an awareness of what's out there and a little more self-control. They're banking on itchy clicker fingers.

---

[75] https://threatpost.com/spotify-phishers-hijack-music-fans-accounts/139329/

Getting Your Teen Talking

Throughout this chapter and in many places throughout the book, I mention the power and benefits of conversation with your kids. Easier said than done, right?

> You: Hey, how was your day?
> Your Teen: Good.
> You: What went on in school today?
> Your Teen: Nothing.
> You: Hey, want to go to the ramen restaurant?
> Your Teen: Whatever.

Yes, it's the world of one-word answers. Sometimes one-syllable answers.

> Your Teen: Yeah.

So how you do break through that and start a discussion about some of these heavyweight topics we've been talking about? Or any topic? One of the first things to realize (and you likely know this if you're the parent of a teen, or if you can simply think back to your own teen years with some degree of clarity) is that those tight lips aren't a symptom of having nothing to say. Teens have plenty to say. Their inner worlds spin with thought, not to mention that the physiology of their brains is still developing. In short, there's someone in there! Complex, conflicted, and just trying to figure themselves out. And that person needs to talk. It can just take a little coaxing to bring them out.

With that in mind, give the following "Seven Ways to Spark Conversation with Your Teen" a try as suggested by my colleague in family safety, Toni Birdsong. She's a parent as well, so she's been there. Her conversation-starters include:

1. Ask open-ended questions. *Stay away from questions that can be answered with "yes" or "no." Instead of asking "Did you have a good day at school?" consider asking "So what was the funniest thing that happened at school today?" (Change out funniest with worst, coolest, or weirdest.)*

2. *Connect with their passion.* *If you can start a conversation with a topic that is of special interest to your teen, you can easily introduce other topics that you want or need to discuss. I often ask my very artistic son, "So what are you working on this week?" and follow up with, "So what inspired that theme in your work?"*

3. *Stop talking and listen.* *You can use a dozen fail-proof strategies to get your teen to open up more, but if you don't listen you will soon be back to one-word answers. Listening without interrupting tells the person speaking that your desire is to understand how they feel or what they think. Genuine listening builds trust, which is gold between a parent and child.*

4. *Feed in small bites.* *Teen attention spans tend to be short, so keep it simple. Don't flood your son or daughter with multiple topics or questions at once. Likewise, know when to wrap it up before a good conversation becomes a lecture. Learn to appreciate the gift of regular dialogue with your teen. Remember, your son or daughter's brain is not calibrated to match your enthusiasm on certain topics, so be wise and manage your expectations.*

5. *Learn to add humor.* *In my experience, teens are slow to trust or open up to adults who don't know how to laugh. Whenever possible, bring a light-hearted spirit to your conversations. Pepper your everyday banter with randomness and goofy observations and don't be afraid to risk looking silly. You can also find common ground in television comedies your son or daughter enjoys. I once taped a whole season of* The Colbert Report *and* The Office *because my then seventeen-year-old was such a big fan. I am now a Colbert and Office convert and use dialogue or expressions from the shows to connect with my son.*

6. *Take advantage of drive time.* *Sometimes sitting down face-to-face can be intimidating or make a teen censor his or her thoughts before speaking. But when eye contact isn't required words tend to flow more freely. When my kids were younger, I used to wait until bedtime to talk. Almost on cue, once the lights were out, both my son and daughter opened up more. Now that they are older, the car seems to do the trick. The best conversations now happen on the drive to/from school or simply running errands.*

7. *Play the high-low game.* *I've saved my favorite for last. We've played "high-low" with our kids since they were old enough to talk. We simply go around the table at dinnertime (or after story time when they were young) and* *play "high-low." One by one, each member of the family shares the high (the best) part of their day and then the low (the worst) part of their day. It's amazing what significant information is shared that could easily have slipped by unspoken. Often a brief "high-low" answer expands into a much longer story or dialogue.*[76]

I love these suggestions, partly because they conjure up memories of conversations I had with my kids when they were teenagers. (That time in the car example is a big one.) I think Toni really nailed it because of how informal these examples are. They're moments you can pepper into any day. Just be ready to catch that chatty moment when it falls into your lap. The times when your teen will open up can really surprise you—in a good way.

What Did We Learn?

We certainly packed plenty into this chapter, didn't we? No surprise, the teen years are some big years, for parents and kids alike.

As we look at it all through a digital lens, we note that so much hinges on when a kid gets his or her first smartphone. With a smartphone, the internet becomes persistent and mobile—it's always on and always nearby, which opens all manner of positive possibilities and potential pitfalls for teens. Our job here is to help our teens develop a well-adjusted relationship with the internet, even when that presents a challenge. After all, with a smartphone, we're no longer peeking over their shoulder from time to time while they're online like we did when they were younger.

Eventually, teens will more than likely get their first smartphone somewhere during this stage of life. Again, there are many opinions as to when it's the "right" time to give your child a smartphone, yet I believe there are no absolutes here. The answer resides in what works well for you, your child, your family, and your situation, just as I outlined earlier in this chapter. I hope you find what I've written on this topic helpful. After all, it's a big decision that prompts more than a fair share of consideration and preparation before the time is

---

[76] https://securingtomorrow.mcafee.com/consumer/family-safety/7-creative-ways-get-teen-talking/

indeed "right." Just as you won't automatically hand over your car keys to your kid when they turn 16 or 17, you won't necessarily be handing over a smartphone at whatever age they request one.

From there, we talked plenty about topics ranging from cyberbullying, friends, gaming, "secret" lives online, and even a bit about impulse control in teens as it relates to becoming a victim of cybercrime. The common thread that runs through them all is you—your presence and your guidance. You can opt to employ some of the technology-driven solutions I've outlined so far, like setting up parental controls and having access to your child's social media account when they first get started with that. Just be aware that none of those solutions are effective on their own without you.

You'll find that some of the best protection you provide stems from conversations. By sitting down with them while they play an online game, asking them about what apps they like using, having them give you a look at that Instagram photo that's making them laugh while they glance at their phone, or using any other such prompt, you can get a glimpse into their digital life and gain some understanding of what they have going on there. In all, keep a sharp eye on moods and feelings when they're online. Together, they provide cues as to when and where you may want or need to step in, support them, and keep them on the right path.

5

AGES 18 TO 24 – ENTERING THE ADULT WORLD

Maybe you were like me and had your share of board games in the house as a kid. Monopoly was a family staple, as were raucous games of pinochle. The Game of Life was yet another favorite—remember that one? Its big board featured roads on which you'd drive a little six-seater station wagon, propelled by spins of the dial that told you how many spaces to go. As you traversed plastic mountains and bridges, life events would occur You'd go to school, get a job, get married, pay taxes, have kids, and eventually end the game by driving up a final stretch of road—right up to the doorstep of your new grand mansion. Just like real life, right? (Grand mansion not included.) Well, not exactly.

Now you're living your actual life and you have a young adult who's about to jump into the real world with both feet, away from the presence of your direct and guiding hand. In the Game of Life, they'd have their own little station wagon and be moving in a random yet orderly way into the adult world. One thing, though: Our kids each take their own path into adulthood. There's no single track through the plastic mountains. It's a winding road with plenty of forks from big decisions and responsibilities that'll take them in this direction or that.

Quite often there's a transition period as our kids get up on their own two feet. For example, they might get some financial support from you if they go on to college or take on a trade; you might find they need to piggyback on your health insurance for their first few years in the workforce (as you know, that stuff is expensive!); or you might be sending off regular care packages as they're serving overseas. Beyond that, you may continue to support them in other ways as they enter young adulthood. They'll still look to you for guidance and advice as they establish themselves. Your kids will need to set up bank accounts, credit cards, and insurance plans of their own—and, another biggie, file their taxes. It's only natural that you'll want to help them make smart choices as they navigate all of that.

As you look back at your own experience as a young adult, much of this likely sounds familiar. However, today's parents (that's you) might add the use of technology to the list of things they'll need support with once they're out of the house.

Then again, your kids are on the leading edge of technology adoption. To some degree, they've grown up in an online and on-demand world of digital. If anyone was "born to share," it's kids who can be grouped as millennials, Gen Zers, and so forth. We've watched the internet rise around us, seemingly developing itself as it delivers access to untold goodness and more than its fair share of bad things. Our kids, well, they take it for granted, just like we took things such as 52 channels of cable TV for granted when we were growing up. (When I was a kid, we had four stations. Memories.) It's been an ever-present part of their lives. As a result, they hop onto new technology bandwagons more readily than the rest of us, and they'll tell you as much. According to Nielsen:

> *In fact, when asked what makes their generation unique, Millennials ranked "Technology Use" first (24%), followed by "Music/Pop Culture" (11%) and "Liberal/Tolerant" (7%). In contrast, Boomers ranked "Work Ethic" as the most defining characteristic of their generation.[77]*

---

[77] https://www.nielsen.com/us/en/insights/news/2014/millennials-technology-social-connection.html

Unsurprisingly, you'll see that reflected in smartphone ownership as well:

More than nine-in-ten Millennials (92%) own smartphones, compared with 85% of Gen Xers (those who turn ages 38 to 53 this year), 67% of Baby Boomers (ages 54 to 72) and 30% of the Silent Generation (ages 73 to 90), according to a new analysis of Pew Research Center data.[78]

You've probably seen all of this in action. At this age, your kids are buying all kinds of connected things: laptops, wireless speakers, and connected cameras, and maybe a gaming console, to name a few. On top of that, you've also seen their enthusiasm for new apps and digital-enabled services: ridesharing apps, carsharing apps, scooter-sharing apps, bike-sharing apps, and so on. (At least they can get around like never before!)

So, while we're active participants in the online world, our adult-age kids drive it in many respects. As new apps and internet-powered services enter the marketplace, they're often ready and willing to give them a try before we do. It's probably safe to say that they hear about them long before we do too, and that we often look to them for advice on the latest and greatest connected thing or app. They're plugged in that way; and perhaps they're wired that way, given the world they grew up in. Our "born to share" babies have grown up.

Given that our adult kids are likely a couple of steps ahead of us (and because they're hopefully out of the house), their safety and privacy online may feel a bit out of our hands. And that's true, up to a point. But, even if they're already on their own or they're well on their way, you still have plenty of opportunities to help them continue to build good habits.

Keeping them Close after They've Left the Nest

Back when they were younger and still at home, you couldn't prepare them for everything that would happen to them on the

---

[78] http://www.pewresearch.org/fact-tank/2018/05/02/millennials-stand-out-for-their-technology-use-but-older-generations-also-embrace-digital-life/

playground or in school, but you did numerous things that prepared them in a general way and rounded them out as a whole person. You instilled in them notions of what's right and wrong, a sense of etiquette and empathy, and simply common sense and good rules to live by. Those things got them through childhood, thanks in large part to you. Now you can support them as young adults in much the same way. Just as you're there to lend a hand or give some good advice in life matters, you can do the same for technology and online services too.

For starters, let's talk about a few concrete things you can do for them as they become young adults:

Continue to be their friend and follower in social media. You may have established a few digital friendships with your kid via different social media platforms while he or she was a teen, and you'll probably keep that up now. It gives you not only another way to stay close to them but also a little insight into how they're handling situations with others. Let's face it, sometimes sticky situations in daily life have a way of spilling over into social media—and vice versa. Not that you'll want to nose into their business at every turn, of course, but being their friend online provides another opportunity to offer your support if and when it makes sense.

Support them as they continue to manage their finances online. This is a big one, and maybe you and your kid have already taken your first steps toward this while they were a teen at home. Managing finances and banking by way of apps and online services is the norm nowadays. There are plenty of checks that can get deposited with a snap of an app, plus services like PayPal and Venmo that allow for making and sharing payments with friends (like splitting the bill at dinner or paying rent). Helping them keep all of this straight now sets them up for future success, particularly as the internet increasingly becomes the window to their financial world— a notion that's reinforced by this finding from Nielsen:

But Millennials aren't just using technology to connect with friends. Their comfort level with digital has them engaging online in ways other generations are just warming up to. For example, Millennials like to handle their finance themselves, and they primarily do so online. And their savvy extends beyond

92

balancing their check books. Older Millennials are 28 percent more likely than average to buy mutual funds online. And, both younger and older Millennials are more likely than their older counterparts to engage in online trading. They're also the heaviest Internet bankers and most likely to purchase insurance online.[79]

Help them to establish and monitor credit and their accounts. Earlier in the book, we talked about freezing your child's credit at birth, given that fraudsters see young children's identities as prime targets for identity theft and fraud. By 18 to 24 years old, chances are good that your kid has a growing credit history of their own. So, there's no better time to make sure they know about the importance of monitoring their rating from the three major credit reporting agencies in the U.S. (Equifax, Experian, and TransUnion).

Turns out, we got a bit of a shock on this count in our household when my daughter was a sophomore in college. Since she had a steady income because she worked while she went to school, my daughter knew she needed to file her income tax return. She loaded up TurboTax on her laptop and completed a 1040EZ in no time at all, excited about the prospect of getting a $600 tax return. (Every dollar counts when you're a student.) But when she attempted to file, she was notified that her taxes had already been filed. What a surprise! Thinking she would never see her refund and having no idea what to do, she reached out to her mom and dad. (Fortunately for her, this was not our first rodeo. More on that later.) It took six months, but we were able to get everything sorted out and get her refund. We also took steps to freeze her credit in case the identity thief tried something else. Today she has a great credit score and has not seen any further evidence that her identity has been used for other fraudulent activities.

A GOBankingRates article shares some additional great insights on how to prevent tax refund fraud. [80] For example, never respond to an email, text or social media contact claiming to be from the IRS. The IRS only initiates contact with taxpayers by postal mail. The

---

[79] https://www.nielsen.com/us/en/insights/news/2014/millennials-technology-social-connection.html
[80] https://www.gobankingrates.com/taxes/refunds/how-to-protect-tax-refund/#.XGa08ib3xEs.twitter

same goes for calls from anyone claiming to represent the IRS. If either happens to you, report it. You can do so at the IRS Impersonation Scam Reporting website. You've earned your tax refund. It's important that you're able to enjoy it without any hassle. Following the steps outlined in the article will go a long way toward allowing you to avoid problems.

Keep the conversation going. Both of my kids proudly serve in the military. My son is a captain in the Marine Corps and my daughter is a captain in the Army. Throughout the years, the military has served up warnings about terrorist organizations using social media to understand movements of people in the armed services in an effort to target them. So we have had regular discussions about steps they should take to make sure they don't broadcast their movements and to keep details about where they live out of the public eye. You should consider your kid's occupation and determine what additional security and privacy measures they can take to maintain a distinction between their professional and personal lives, which can keep them safer and more private as well.

Keep an eyeball on your shared accounts. My kids still use my Amazon Prime and Netflix accounts, but pretty much everything else is their own at this point. I suspect that many families take this hybrid approach in an effort to help their kids better manage their finances and to take full advantage of the subscription options available to them. Just check your account for activity to make sure that only your family circle is using your accounts. For example, my daughter-in-law recently used my Amazon Prime account to buy a gift for a friend. When I saw a new address in my Amazon account, I instantly sent her a text message to see if it was legit. It was and all was well.

Keep them on the family's security software plan. It's common for security software to include licenses for multiple numbers of PCs, Macs, smartphones, and tablets that are part of the same household. One purchase can cover your whole family, even if they are not living at home all the time. The more comprehensive packages out there are a great choice because what they offer goes well beyond basic antivirus protection. They can look after your privacy, help you keep tabs on your social media profiles, guard against identity theft, and much more.

Let's Talk About Finances Again: Sending Money Online

First off, you can send money to people easier than before; where we once cut checks or forked over cash when we were their age, today's young adults use digital payment apps to settle up. As mentioned above, they use them to reimburse each other for rent, split dinner, or score concert tickets. And now adults share payments much the same way. Like a lot of people, I play Fantasy Football. The $20 buy-in is made using PayPal to the commissioner's email address. Easy peasy. Digital payment apps running on our smartphones make taking care of a payment just as quick as taking out a wallet, with the convenience of not having to carry all that cash around. (Or make change.) Popular apps include the aforementioned PayPal and Venmo, along with Cash App and Zelle—popular to the point of an estimated $700 billion transferred in the U.S. in 2018.[81] In 2017, nearly two-thirds of millennials sent or received money with these apps.[82]

Indeed, these apps work like a digital wallet, where you can link your app to your bank account, credit card, or debit card. You can also carry a balance in your digital payment account and simply draw funds from there. Transfers between sender and recipient can take seconds, although sometimes transactions can get flagged for review and take longer to conduct.

On the subject of flags and lags in payment: this issue came up with Venmo, which is owned by PayPal, in a complaint settled by the U.S. Federal Trade Commission (FTC) in 2018. It was alleged that Venmo misrepresented available funds to users, such that when a user received notification of payment, Venmo stated that the funds received were ready to be transferred to a bank account, if the user wished. This allegedly was not the case. "That's because Venmo

---

[81] https://www.consumer.ftc.gov/blog/2018/02/tips-using-peer-peer-payment-systems-and-apps
[82] https://www.chicagotribune.com/business/success/kiplinger/tca-peer-to-peer-payments-carry-risks-20180420-story.html

waited until a consumer attempted to transfer funds to his or her external bank account to review the transaction for fraud, insufficient funds, or other problems. For many consumers, once Venmo undertook that review, it resulted in delaying the transfer or even reversing the transaction altogether."[83] As a result, a proposed order from the FTC required PayPal to clearly disclose when transactions are subject to review and that funds could be frozen or removed. Another aspect of the complaint was that Venmo allegedly made it difficult for users *not to publicly share* records of their transactions on Venmo's platform feed and on the user's personal profile page, where their most recent transactions were posted. The proposed order thus added, "In addition, PayPal must provide clear disclosures about how any payment and social networking service shares transaction information with other users and must tell consumers how to adjust privacy settings to limit how that information is shared."[84] So if you or your kid use these apps, be sure to double-check that your deposits went through and check to see if there are any privacy settings involved, as in the case of Venmo. It also helps to turn notifications on so whenever a transaction or other activity takes place you know about it instantly.

And because we're talking about a combination of money and the internet, keep an eyeball out for scammers who use the anonymity of the internet to their advantage. In a *Chicago Tribune* article, Rivan V. Stinson, a reporter at *Kiplinger's Personal Finance* magazine, explained it this way:

> *But as the use of these apps grows, so do complaints about scams. The Federal Trade Commission added online payment systems to its complaint database last year, and more complaints about scams are appearing on social media sites. The schemes are similar: Someone pretends to be selling, say, concert tickets, dupes victims into sending money and then disappears.*

---

[83] https://www.ftc.gov/news-events/blogs/business-blog/2018/02/venmo-settlement-addresses-availability-funds-privacy
[84] https://www.ftc.gov/news-events/blogs/business-blog/2018/02/venmo-settlement-addresses-availability-funds-privacy
[81] https://www.chicagotribune.com/business/success/kiplinger/tca-peer-to-peer-payments-carry-risks-20180420-story.html

Consumers have come to expect some form of protection when they link their bank accounts or debit cards to these apps. But when you're using electronic forms of payment to make a purchase from another individual — instead of a traditional merchant — the rules are different and there's less protection against fraud, says Sarah Grotta of Mercator Advisory Group.[85]

The rules, as they stand today, go like this: if you send funds using a "friends and family" option, it's a person-to-person (P2P) transaction that you authorized, and thus you're not covered for losses. Stinson goes on to reiterate the need for care and caution when using digital apps for these transactions:

Venmo, owned by PayPal, states in its user agreement that personal accounts are meant to be used only between family and friends. Its definition of what's considered an unauthorized transaction is similar to PayPal's. The same goes for Cash.

Zelle, another P2P app, looks like a safer bet because it's backed by big banks, such as Chase, Citi and Wells Fargo. But banks that have integrated Zelle into their systems stress that the app is for sending money to someone you know. If you do business with strangers and get scammed, you're likely out of luck.[86]

Financial technology (fintech) apps are all the rage right now. "Fintech is the new technology and innovation that aims to compete with traditional financial methods in the delivery of financial services. It is an emerging industry that uses technology to improve activities in finance. The use of smartphones for mobile banking, investing services and cryptocurrency are examples of technologies aiming to make financial services more accessible to the general public."[87] Fintech can offer great conveniences, such as investment apps like Robinhood that allow you to buy and sell stock without paying fees and round-up apps like Acorns that round up your credit card transaction to the nearest dollar and invest the round up amount. However, you need to keep in mind that these apps require access to your bank account and credit cards. Before using these

---

[86] Ibid.
[87] https://en.wikipedia.org/wiki/Financial_technology

types of apps make sure they have a healthy number of downloads along with a high rating and customer reviews. Also, carefully monitor any credit cards or bank accounts tied to these apps for suspicious transactions.

Again, all of what I'm writing here covers things to keep in mind as you use these fantastic conveniences so you can undertake your transactions with a clear understanding of how they work and what any potential issues are. If you're wondering if I use them, I sure do. In a nutshell, here's an outstanding summary of how to go about it, courtesy of one of my colleagues in security, Radhika Sarang:

- **Make sure the computers and devices that use these apps on are secure.** At the very least, start with a strong and secure password for your accounts. Then there are pros and cons of biometric (fingerprint, facial recognition or retinal scan) protection. But, if you can, opt for two-factor authentication as well. "Two-factor authentication (also known as 2FA) is a type, or subset, of multi-factor authentication. It is a method of confirming users' claimed identities by using a combination of two different factors: 1) something they know, 2) something they have, or 3) something they are."[88] Although not foolproof, two-factor authentication is significantly more secure than just relying on a user name and password. Be sure to use it whenever possible.

- **Update your systems and the apps that run on them regularly.** Developers are always addressing potential and known security issues. This is a rule of thumb for all your apps. Updates provide an extra line of defense against hackers and fraud.

- **Be careful what you click on.** Seventy-one percent of cyberattacks start with a phishing email where someone sends a link baiting someone to take an action. (We will cover phishing attacks in more detail toward the end of the next chapter.)

- **Confirm that your transactions go through as planned.** If you're transferring to another individual, check in with

---

[88] https://en.wikipedia.org/wiki/Multi-factor_authentication

them to make sure they received their payment. Look at your online bank statement to see if money you sent from your payment app made it into your account.

- **Watch out for scammers when buying tickets or items online.** Again, these are considered P2P transactions, which are not at all protected in the same way when you buy from a merchant. When in doubt, go old school for payments to people who you don't know or trust. Things like exchanging cash for a concert ticket at a coffee shop where there are other folks around will still get the job done.

- **Steer clear of public Wi-Fi** (coffee shops, airports, hotels, and so forth) when you use these apps, banking apps, or any app that passes along sensitive personal or financial information. They're simply not secure. Vulnerabilities in public Wi-Fi networks can make it easy for fraudsters to hack into your transactions and steal information.[89] If you need to use public Wi-Fi be sure to connect using a virtual private network (VPN) application. Using a VPN will create an encrypted tunnel from your device to the internet and help keep your traffic from prying eyes. (See "The Family CIO Checklist" in chapter 6 for more details about what a VPN is and how to shop around for one that's right for you and your family.)

Digital Adulting

Now that they're out on their own, our children will start doing more adult things and will learn what life looks like beyond the shelter of our wings. Some will embrace this newfound freedom and take flight right away, while others will need to be nudged out of the nest. (Or kicked.) Whether they go boldly into this new world or take tepid steps, they'll need to prepare themselves for a life of adulting. Digitally speaking, there are a few ways you can give them a solid start.

I touched on identity theft of children earlier in the book and the importance of locking your child's identity down as soon as possible.

---

[89] https://securingtomorrow.mcafee.com/consumer/mobile-and-iot-security/sending-money-over-mobile-devices/

However, your child's identity really starts to take shape and become a focal point to thieves and fraudsters at this stage of their lives and as they get older. The more value we create in our lives the more someone will want to try to take it from us, so your young adult will want to take ownership of their identity. Earlier in this chapter I talked about my daughter's experience of having an identity thief submit a fraudulent tax return with her identity. She is very easygoing about things in general and was sure that her mom and dad would sort things out, but the experience still took an emotional toll. Should something similar happen to your kid, there will be moments when they will think that all is lost and find it tough to get on with their life. If they are victims of any crime, be it physical or cyber in nature, it's important that we support them in any way possible. Comfort them and assure them that while cleaning up such a mess requires a lot of work, you're willing and able to help.

We often think of identity theft as something financial in nature. Someone uses our private information to get a credit card as us or submit a fraudulent tax return. That is often the case, but more and more thieves are targeting other aspects of our identity that hold value as well. For example, your kid will embark on travels of his or her own and will likely gravitate toward a favorite airline or hotel chain. Like the rest of us, they'll join a loyalty program and start accumulating points for discounts and dream trips. And there's a good reason why we are seeing more and more instances of cyberthieves targeting these loyalty accounts. According to CreditCards.com there are billions of dollars at risk, "Loyalty plan earnings are compelling targets because thieves can monetize them in different ways. One shady seller on the underground forum Darknet Markets advertises American Airlines miles and Hilton points, which, the seller explains, buyers can sell to online mileage brokers; redeem for physical gift cards, electronics and other merchandise through the issuers' online shopping malls; use to book flights and hotel stays; and exchange via points exchange site Points.com for different program miles or points." [90]

---

[90] https://www.creditcards.com/credit-card-news/crooks-target-rewards-points-1277.php

Because the points earned in these programs are worth real dollars, encourage your child to treat their loyalty accounts the same way they treat bank accounts (i.e., use two-factor authentication wherever available, monitor account activity, use strong and unique passwords for each account, enable notifications, respond to alerts, and report suspicious activity).

Another major step along the path to digital adulthood is reputation management. And in today's world, that means your kids need to clean up their pictures and posts on social media. At the time, that picture of an empty 12-pack of Schmidt on your head may have seemed like a pretty good post to your kid. (Tons of people gave it a thumbs up!) However, pictures like that will linger online if they aren't taken down, and they could have real-world consequences when your kid is up for a new job or promotion. Photos, remarks, or other actions that may cause them reputation harm need to get scrubbed. I know this may take a while because they have been flooding their data lake for years now, but it could save them future heartache and frustration. Likewise, have your kids look out for their friends. None of us will always make the smartest choices. Not every picture of every not-so-great moment needs to get posted and shared with the world. The earlier advice of stop and think before you post still applies here.

During this stage of life, your child will start building their professional network and will likely use social media platforms such as LinkedIn to make connections, post their resume, and perhaps share some of their accomplishments. Naturally there's a clear distinction between what's posted on Facebook and LinkedIn, so they'll want to pay close attention to privacy settings and any links between the various social media platforms. For example, I link my LinkedIn profile to my Twitter account since I use both for communicating as a professional. However, I keep Facebook separate. That's for my personal life and thus reserved for friends and family. When you talk with your child about the pros and cons of the different social media platforms, make sure you talk about audiences. Who's seeing this? What kind of relationship do they have with you? Are you clear about the things you want and don't want to share with them? When you help your kids look at social media through lenses such as those, it's much easier for them to determine what makes the most sense for them.

Online Dating

If we can equate popularity with dollars, online dating is high on the list of online activities. In the U.S. alone, online dating is on pace to drum up $1.2 billion according to Statista, an online statistics portal. Of course, that's not from young adults alone. You or someone you know may have met someone through online dating since the first dating site, Match.com, hit the scene in the mid-1990's. So let's just say there's a fair chance your kid may turn to a dating service or dating app to simply meet more people or on his or her quest to find "the one."

I'll start out by saying that online dating has come a long way in 20 years. The reputable services like OkCupid, eHarmony, and Match.com each offer privacy settings and features that put people in control of managing who sees their profile, who can contact them, and how. This is vital in an age of cyberstalkers (see the previous chapter) and people with generally ill intent who troll the internet for victims. Another concern is that dating sites collect a treasure trove of personal information about their users, obviously with the intent of helping people find a match. That makes dating profiles particularly attractive in lawsuits and legal situations, which further makes them subject to seizure by court order. And if a profile is attractive to courts and lawyers, it's also attractive to hackers. A breach in a dating site could expose a person's name, where they live, their email, their message history, their dating browsing history, and on and on. Again, any privacy-minded person should consider these issues when they look to meet other people with these services.

With these things in mind, I'll offer up some top-level advice that you can pass along: play it extra safe and sane. All the things I've mentioned before about social media still apply but are amped up a couple notches and with a few additions. Feel free to share what follows with your kid. And if you're a single parent, feel free to take this advice too.

Protecting your privacy when dating online begins with setting up your account. Don't link any of your existing accounts to it at all. That means creating a new email address just for this account, a fresh username you don't use elsewhere, and an entirely new phone number that you can get through Google Voice, Burner, Hushed, or Flyp. (For more on getting a second number, check out the CNET article that I've footnoted here.[91]) This puts up a privacy firewall between you and the dating world. Should something go sideways in your dating account, your core personal information and points of contact won't be affected by a breach, a creep, or some other unforeseen circumstance.

You'll also want to play it cool. Be slow and deliberate in your responses when a person shows interest in you, and don't be afraid to say NO if they're pressing you for details you don't want to share. After all, it will take some time before you get to truly know who is on the other side of that dating profile, let alone if they are someone you can trust (which is kind of the point if you are serious about dating).

For a more detailed checklist of what folks should consider when using a dating app or website, this excerpt from an article posted on ASECURELIFE.com offers tips in three areas:[92]

1. **Choosing a site and setting up your profile**
   - Avoid sites and apps that let just anyone message you.
   - Pay attention to the geography settings in dating apps.
   - Use unique photos for your dating profile.
   - Avoid putting lots of personal details on your profile.
2. **Interacting online**
   - Use the dating app's messaging system.
   - Set up a Google Voice phone number just for dating.
   - Talk to mutual friends.

---

[91] https://www.cnet.com/how-to/apps-that-give-your-phone-a-second-number/
[92] https://www.asecurelife.com/online-dating-safety/

- Get to know them, but don't share too many details at first.

3. **Meeting in the real world**
   - Arrange your own transportation.
   - Meet in a public place for your first date.
   - Stay aware and alert.
   - Enlist the help of a friend.
   - Keep some emergency cash on hand.
   - Consider carrying a self-defense tool.

I admit that I was a little struck by the mention of a self-defense tool, yet that doesn't need to be a set of brass knuckles or a sock full of wood screws. It could be pepper spray or some other deterrent. Heck, it could be that you're trained in self-defense. The point is, once again, it will take some time before you have a true sense of who your suitor is. Play it smart and be prepared to protect yourself.

One last thing that comes to mind with dating apps, which echoes advice I mentioned in the section about cyberstalkers, is to turn off any location-finding functionality in your dating app. Telegraphing your presence at this location or that to strangers only invites trouble. Remember: play it extra safe and sane.

Their Data Lake Just Got a Whole Lot Deeper

With all the apps that connect adults to digitally driven services (including Uber, Lyft, Bird scooters, Lime bikes, vacation rentals, sharing vehicles, and even timesharing workspaces), you can sure bet that your kid's data lake will fill up with all kinds of data with an almost audible rush. In there, you'll find data about their travels and how they spend their time, as well as a lot of their other online activities (the same ones you do), such as managing finances, filing insurance claims, ordering items from online retailers, and much more. It's quite possible that their data lake is growing faster than yours.

We'll take a close look at what data lakes *really* look like in the next chapter, with an (*ahem*) deep dive into how they fill up so quickly, so that you can exercise some degree of control over what's going in there.

What Did We Learn?

We support our kids in many ways as they make the transition to newly minted young adult and in the years after that as they get set up in the world. This support may or may not take a financial form, but it always has an emotional and practical dimension to it. As you know, your kids still benefit from your presence in their lives—even as they're pulling away in their radically different counterparts to that plastic station wagon in the Game of Life. You have plenty to share even as they build their own lives on their own terms. You're their sounding board when they have a lousy day. You're their font of worldly advice about how things work. You're their parent. Still. And always. You can stay as involved in this fashion as the two of you both see fit, and it's good to know that the digital world is one of many ways you can continue to connect and keep close.

6

AGES 25 TO 54 – YOUR BRIMMING DATA LAKE

It's too bad that no sound gets made when someone or something captures personal data from you. Like a ping or a chime. Maybe it's just as well. We'd never hear anything else above the clatter and din.

Because we can't truly see, hear, or immediately sense how and where this data capture is occurring, it's difficult at first to realize just how pervasive it is. Moreover, visualizing what's done with that data once a website, app, or service collects it is just as difficult too, if not more so. For example, what's being done with the data you generate when you use a discount club card at your supermarket, when you post on social media, when you install a smart thermostat in your house, when you use a fitness tracking app, when you install one of those "safe driver" monitoring devices for lower auto insurance rates, or any number of other connected devices or services that use your personal data and promise some benefit or discount in return? The answer: it depends.

Those So-Called Free Apps Come with a Cost

The same answer seems to hold true about American attitudes about the balance between their privacy and disclosure of personal information when using websites, apps, and services online: it depends.[93] The internet and our phones are loaded with plenty of "free" offerings that aren't exactly free at all. There's still an exchange that takes place as you use them. No cash passes hands; instead, you pass along something just as valuable—your personal information or information about your habits and behaviors. I'm not exactly sure who first coined the phrase, but "the real cost of free" sums up the issue well. It offers a shorthand way to describe the "economic and consumer concerns around apps and websites that collect and track data about you in exchange for providing you a service free of cost."[94] That supermarket discount card is a good example. You share your purchasing history with the supermarket chain and you get a discount on the good stuff in your cart. The supermarket chain then gets insight into your shopping habits, along with data that they could, potentially, share with others.

Welcome to the new world of data and privacy, brought to you by the internet and the commercial interests that shape it. We'll take a square and level look at it in this chapter.

Whether we're using a free app or simply going about our daily lives with a smartphone at our side and a laptop on our desk, this is the age where we're generating our greatest volumes of data daily. Recall from an earlier chapter that today we consume about 650 megabytes of data per day, which will rise to 1.5 gigabytes of data over the next couple of years. What's more, this data is of high quality and high interest to good and bad actors alike because it comprises information about our health, our finances, our credit rating, our comings, our goings, and on and on. This has value to insurers, to marketing and operations arms in large corporations, to all manner of financial professionals, and, sadly, to crooks. This is the world in which we live now. Everyone who uses the internet and

---

[93] http://www.pewinternet.org/2016/01/14/privacy-and-information-sharing/

[94] https://curriculum.code.org/csp-1718/unit4/4/

everyone who has a child who uses the internet needs to understand this new reality and act upon it in a manner that they see fit. Code.org frames this situation as follows:

> *Many consumers are unaware, or lack a sophisticated understanding, of how information about us is being collected and tracked by the technology we use every day. This issue goes beyond instances when data is stolen from companies or organizations we willingly provide it to. Instead, using computational tools, our movements through the physical and virtual world are being automatically tracked, stored, and analyzed. Cookies in our browsers keep a record of our movements on the Internet. Companies trade access to free tools and apps for the rights to track the data we upload to them. Advertisers develop personalized profiles of potential customers to better target advertising. Governments monitor traffic across the Internet at scales unimaginable without the use of computers. Yet we live in a world that increasingly relies on these digital tools, services and products. Most companies make great efforts to balance the tradeoffs between utility and privacy, but the issues can be tricky and raise confounding ethical dilemmas. We must now grapple with a question of just how much we value our privacy, and whether it is even possible to maintain in a digitized world.[95]*

Another factor in this data equation is the presence of third parties in the mix. That data you generate by using a website, service, or app can get shared with different companies and parties for marketing purposes, research purposes, and the like. This data may or may not be anonymized, meaning stripped of information that could personally identify you. It then gets added into a vast "vat" of anonymized data that's been extracted from other people and can then be shared with companies or organizations for the purposes of extracting insights and trends. Or it may not get shared at all. That all depends on the terms and conditions you agreed to when you used that site or service or clicked yes to that 27-screen-long agreement before you started using an app.

Are your eyes rolling around your head at the thought? Mine are! All those sites, services, and apps we use. Who can keep up with all those user agreements and what's in them? Meanwhile, we go on clicking yes because we believe we're getting some value out of the exchange when we swap our data for the "free" use of an app or

---

[95] Ibid.

service. And not to be at all cynical, plenty of apps and services do give us good things in return—like a record of our fitness, diet, and health; ways of communicating with family, friends, and associates; and games that pass the time—you can just check your phone and find plenty of free apps that either are or could be a welcome part of your daily routine!

It's taken a while, yet according to a Pew Research Center study published in 2016, people are catching on to "the real cost of free," and that they're starting to make savvier decisions based on the data and privacy costs of using free apps:

> *People's views on the key tradeoff of the modern, digital economy – namely, that consumers offer information about themselves in exchange for something of value – are shaped by both the conditions of the deal and the circumstances of their lives. In extended comments online and through focus groups, people indicated that their interest and overall comfort level depends on the company or organization with which they are bargaining and how trustworthy or safe they perceive the firm to be. It depends on what happens to their data after they are collected, especially if the data are made available to third parties. And it also depends on how long the data are retained.[96]*

As you can imagine, this research found that people's attitudes about different types of data and value exchanges vary greatly. For example, the researchers put forward this scenario to participants in their study: "A new health information website is being used by your doctor's office to help manage patient records. Your participation would allow you to have access to your own health records and make scheduling appointments easier. If you choose to participate, you will be allowing your doctor's office to upload your health records to the website and the doctor promises it is a secure site." Interestingly, 52% off people overall perceived this as "Acceptable" with older Americans being more likely to see it as acceptable (62%) versus those who were younger (45%)—the rest said, "It Depends." Contrast that with attitudes about "safe driver discounts" that required the use of a tracking device in their car to monitor speed, location, and general driving habits: overall, 37% found it

---

[96] http://www.pewinternet.org/2016/01/14/privacy-and-information-sharing/

"Acceptable," 45% said "Not Acceptable," and only 16% said "It Depends."

From my own experience, a couple of years ago I owned a brand-new red Corvette. I could not fathom how my driving data would equate to reduced insurance rates. It's an oxymoron in the purest form. One of my friends opted in. He owned a Jeep and had young children at the time. He was a very safe and conscientious driver. He received notices from his insurance company saying that he was going from zero to 60 mph too fast. He lamented that on a good day rolling downhill it would take him about 15 seconds for his Jeep to hit 60, which felt like a very long time. In all, I found the Pew Research Center study fascinating, particularly some of the quotes from the focus group respondents, which ranged anywhere from trusting to guarded to downright skeptical, based on the scenario and their personal outlook. The majority of them seemed like quite real and reasonable points of view when I took a moment to pause and consider them.

That's the key right there I think: pause and consider. Data collection is going to happen. The key is being able to identify when and where it happens, what's being collected, who's using it, how it's being protected, if it's being shared with third parties, and to weigh that against what you know and feel you're getting in return. Put another way—your data is like cash. Are you overpaying for what you're getting? And is this transaction putting you at risk in any way? If you find your eyes rolling around in your head again as I ask these questions, take a deep breath. You're not alone here. The answers are painfully difficult to pin down today.

If Your Data Is Like Cash, Are You Getting Ripped Off?

Case in point, try this quick exercise … think of a few sites, services, or apps that require you to register for an account or to log in. Now try answering the following questions:

1. What kinds of data does (or could) this site potentially collect about you?
2. Do you know if this data is shared with other people, companies, or organizations? (If so, which ones?)

3. Do you know how you would find out what data is collected or how it's shared?[97]

Chances are, you can't rattle off the answers right off the bat. You'll find them hidden in terms and conditions that are written by a company's legal counsel and all too often read like another language. However, some companies have made a conscientious effort to speak as plainly as possible on the topic and now post privacy policy pages that spell out what kind of information is collected, for what purpose, who it's shared with, and so on.

As I write this today, I look back to recent events in the EU and the U.S., where lawmakers have taken on the issue of data collection and sharing in earnest. Lawmakers appear to want what we want—transparency. We want clear answers to all the questions around what organizations can legally collect and share so that we can make informed decisions and protect our privacy.

The EU took a major step in that direction in 2018 when it enacted the GDPR:

The rule, called General Data Protection Regulation or GDPR, focuses on ensuring that users know, understand, and consent to the data collected about them. Under GDPR, pages of fine print won't suffice. Neither will be forcing users to click yes in order to sign up.

Instead, companies must be clear and concise about their collection and use of personal data like full name, home address, location data, IP address, or the identifier that tracks web and app use on smartphones. Companies have to spell out why the data is being collected and whether it will be used to create profiles of people's actions and habits. Moreover, consumers will gain the right to access data companies store about them, the right to correct inaccurate information, and the right to limit the use of decisions made by algorithms, among others.[98]

This should sound like welcome news to you.

---

[97] https://curriculum.code.org/csp-1718/unit4/4/
[98] https://www.wired.com/story/europes-new-privacy-law-will-change-the-web-and-more/

The internet has few borders. For the most part, information flows freely and services are widely available across the globe, so when the GDPR was rolled out, it cast ripples far beyond the European Union. In short, while the law protects people in the 28-member nations of the EU, it also affects the places where their data is processed—even if that's outside of the EU. So tech giants who do business in Europe, like Facebook, Google, and Apple, reacted accordingly. They made updates to privacy settings to make them more clear and accessible to users, and some companies that draw on consumer data and convert it into profit (think large advertisers and data merchants that may not be household names) shut down their European operations out of concern that their businesses were even viable given the new consumer consent requirements (which goes to show how tangled the webs of personal data collection can get). The regulations have teeth, too. Fines of up to 4% of annual global revenue can be levied. Think of what 4% would mean to Google and its 2017 revenue of nearly $110 billion.[99]

For users in the European Union, the GDPR gives them power and control they did not have before. "In short, the law is a chance to flip the economics of the industry. Since the dawn of the commercial web, companies have been financially incentivized to hoover up data and monetize later. Now, EU consumers will have the freedom to opt in, rather than the burden of opting out."[100] An example: imagine droves of people clamping down on their privacy and the data they share or filing requests to have their data removed from sites that data brokers mine for data—well, an entire industry could change.

This is far from over. The GDPR only went into effect in May 2018, just months before I am writing this. There will be challenges, lawsuits, legal questions of jurisdiction, and cases where people and businesses argue the interpretation and practical application of the regulations. The first waves of them are coming now. In January 2019, France's data protection regulator, CNIL, issued Google with

---

[99] https://www.statista.com/statistics/266206/googles-annual-global-revenue/

[100] https://www.wired.com/story/europes-new-privacy-law-will-change-the-web-and-more/

a €50 million fine. Per an article published in The Verge, "CNIL said that the fine was issued because Google failed to provide enough information to users about its data consent policies and didn't give them enough control over how their information is used."[101] Google responded with the promise to review the decision by the French agency to determine how the company will address the concerns and that it would appeal the fine given their concerns "about the impact of this ruling on publishers, original content creators and tech companies in Europe and beyond."[102] Still, examples such as this represent a major step by lawmakers to put consumer protections in place—and to back them with penalties that can truly hurt the businesses and organizations that break the rules. In all, the GDPR sets a precedent. And a global one at that.

Data Collection: Who's Behind It, and What They're Up To

Why is all this transparency and consent so important? It gives you a plain look at the massive amount of data collection and compilation that propels digital business today. You have a cloud of identifiers floating around you in digital space that companies use to track you throughout the day. The device you're using has an ID, an email address/account associated with it, and a phone number if you hop online via a smartphone. From there, like when you shop or handle finances online, your device passes along data like your name, Social Security number, birthday, credit card numbers, and address. You may also have a Google ID for when you use Gmail, YouTube, or other services. Other tech companies have their IDs too, like Apple, Microsoft, Facebook, and Amazon.

Then you have tracking cookies, IP addresses, and device and browser fingerprints—which then get tied to your behaviors, like what sites you visit, what apps you use, what videos you watch, what you buy, and where you go. In addition is the practice of geotracking, where smartphone apps and other devices capture where you are and

---

[101] https://www.theverge.com/2019/1/21/18191591/google-gdpr-fine-50-million-euros-data-consent-cnil
[102] https://www.yahoo.com/news/google-appeal-50-million-euro-french-data-consent-192940250.html

where you go (such as fitness apps that map out your runs around the neighborhood and park or the devices that car insurance companies provide to their customers with the promise of potential good driver discounts) via GPS capabilities. Access to even little wisps of this data you create can tell a company quite a story about you. Thus, regulations like those found in the GDPR can only benefit you by giving you the choice of not only what services to use but also what those services can and can't collect from you. Let's look at that three-question quiz again:

1. What kinds of data does (or could) this site potentially collect about you?
2. Do you know if this data is shared with other people, companies, or organizations? (If so, which ones?)
3. Do you know how you would find out what data is collected or how it's shared?[103]

With the right regulations in place, you could likely answer those questions or even opt out of that data collection altogether—at least, that's the intent.

Now why *would* you opt in for data collection of some kind? Isn't it all bad? You'll find umpteen opinions on that topic. But let me show how some of this data gets used.

Marketing and retail/etail often top the list because we see them the most. At first, you might say, "Ugh. Ads!" However, the other side of the coin is that merchants and stores want to know what you're interested in so they can offer up the ads you'll respond to because they're actually meaningful to you in some way. (They don't always get it right—like when an ad for rice cookers seems to follow you around the internet after you did a search for one online.) But the ad is just the start. That insight then extends to a retailer's inventory, which is no small matter in the case of physical goods. If a retailer knows what you and people like you want, it can stock those items and get them into your hands quickly. In short, data can help you get the stuff you want—or even discover cool things you didn't know you want based on what you have expressed an interest in.

---

[103] https://curriculum.code.org/csp-1718/unit4/4/

Customer data can also lead to better customer service and even to better products. By tracking customer complaints and customer issues that you and others report, creators of products can get a sense of where their offerings have issues. Besides training up staff to handle those complaints, they can stock up on what's needed to remedy those issues (like the parts to re-engineer a doodad or an app update to expunge a snippet of bad computer code) and get data to their design teams so that future products don't have those issues.

Ever get a call from your bank to see if you authorized a debit card payment or not? One reason you get that call is because the bank knows your habits and history. If they suddenly see a purchase that seems a little out of character for you, they'll flag it and reach out to you to ensure you authorized the transaction. And they don't have to be big purchases. A friend of mine got a call from his bank about a few charges for Domino's Pizza. Turns out, they weren't his. In any event, he cancelled his compromised debit card thanks to big data and thin-crust pizza.

There are plenty of other useful examples where data collection and analysis benefits businesses and people like us. What I want to convey is that data collection isn't *always* bad in and of itself. It's how data is collected, shared, and secured where the risks and issues arise.

We already talked about one downside of data collection, where the lack of transparency and consent has given rise to big businesses who are compiling insights from data about our habits, movements, and activities without us truly knowing or understanding what they're doing, and then selling that information for big bucks in aggregated and anonymized form to others. Now let's talk about another issue: security.

2018 was not a good year for Facebook. They took a welter of blows from the public, press, and legislators for data breaches and allegedly questionable data-sharing practices with third parties. In December of that year, Facebook announced that the social network had exposed the private photos of millions of users without their permission.[104] According to Facebook, a bug allowed third-party app developers access to some 6.8 million photos that people may not have shared publicly. Prior to that, Facebook found itself embroiled in revelations about another third-party app developer, Cambridge Analytica, who allegedly used Facebook to gather data on tens of millions of Americans.

I'll set aside finger-wagging and politics here because whatever ends these photos and data are used for are one issue—but the core issue is one of trust. When you use a platform or app or service, your expectation is that your data is secure. Facebook is taking its lumps not only because of its breaches but also because they're such a high-profile brand that people know and use. However, many more companies beyond Facebook failed to protect consumer data in 2018.

Protecting Yourself in the Wake of Big Breaches

In years past, we've seen major data breaches big credit reporting agencies like Equifax and major retailers like Target, which have collectively put millions and millions of instances of personal data and financial records in jeopardy by putting them out in the wild—on the internet. Data security has evolved into, and will remain, a massive issue due to the global scale of its impact on people's lives. Financially speaking, as reported in *Forbes*, "On average, each record costs $148 and a breach of 1 million records costs $40 million while a breach of 50 million costs $350 million. The research also found that the efficiency in identifying an incident and the speed of the response has a huge impact on its overall cost. On average, it took companies 197 days to identify a data breach and 69 days to contain it."[105] And that's just for businesses. Think about what a breach means for the actual people behind each "record." What do they lose when their accounts or identity are compromised? If you've had it happen to you, you know the hours and hours of work it takes to

[104] https://www.cnn.com/2018/12/14/tech/facebook-private-photos-exposed-bug/index.html
[105] https://www.forbes.com/sites/niallmccarthy/2018/07/13/the-average-cost-of-a-data-breach-is-highest-in-the-u-s-infographic/#64ebba0d2f37

clean up after this, and that it can take months or even years to resolve in some of the worst cases. Plus, they can lose money too. Money they may or may not see come back.

I'll share the time this happened to me. The 401K administrator at a company I was working at about 15 years ago sold our personal information (SSN, address, date of birth, etc.) to an identity thief. I recall a Saturday morning when I got "the call."

> Them: Hello, is this Gary Davis?
> Me: Yes.
> Them: Do you live at this address [address withheld]?
> Me: Yes.
> Them: Is your Social Security number 123-456-7890 [actual SSN withheld]?
> Me: Yes.
> Them: Did you recently apply for and receive a credit card from our company, [name withheld]?
> Me: No.

Apparently, the identity thief went to their website and was approved for a credit card with a $20,000 limit in a different state than the one I lived in. That's right, twenty grand! I always wonder why they didn't cap the credit card at $2,000 to get started—especially considering that it was approved without any proof of identity. The credit card company got suspicious when the identity thief ran up charges to $18,000 over the course of one weekend. Back in those days, it was common for thieves to buy high-cost equipment at electronics stores and then return it to a different store for cash. Because the crime was committed in another state, I needed to work with both local law enforcement and the FBI and then sign an affidavit attesting that I had not participated in this in any way. I also immediately froze my credit with all the reporting agencies and had them place a red flag on my credit, an indication of fraud or suspicious activity warning the credit bureaus that they needed to notify me if someone tried to open credit as me.

In a recent *Forbes* article, Liz Frazier Peck covers how U.S. adults are still leaving themselves at risk for continued security breaches:

The potential of a cybercriminal stealing our information is a significant source of stress for many Americans. In fact, more people believe that having their identity stolen would be worse than having their home broken into (46% vs. 27%). So we know it's a problem, we worry about it...yet we still are not protecting our data. A recent study conducted by CreditCards.com found that more than 9 in 10 (92%) U.S. adults have been guilty of at least one risky data security behavior in the past year.

Specific risky behaviors include:

- *More than 8 in 10 (82%) have reused online passwords, including 61% who use the same password at least half of the time and 22% who always do.*
- *Using a public Wi-Fi network (48%)*
- *Saving passwords (45%) and payment info (35%) online*
- *Carrying a Social Security card in a purse or wallet (33%)[106]*

In the "Enter the Family CIO" section later in this chapter, I'll step you through what you can to do avoid each of these risky behaviors—with the exception of carrying your Social Security card in your purse or wallet. The only reason for ever carrying it with you would be the rare instance of having an appointment that will require it, such as getting a new job where an employer is asking to see it. I suggest you only carry it to your appointment and then keep it in a safe place until you need it again. Having misplaced mine and having gone through the process (aka hassle) of getting a new one, trust me when I say it's better off in a secure location instead of in your wallet or purse.

What are companies doing today to fight back to protect themselves, and you, from breaches? Plenty. Most companies have a defense in depth approach where they put layered security solutions in place to protect your data from bad actors. That's not to say that things still don't go wrong. It feels like every day we *hear* about another breach of a well-known company or organization. But the good news is that the topic of cybersecurity continues to be a

---

[106] https://www.forbes.com/sites/lizfrazierpeck/2019/02/07/over-90-of-adults-put-their-personal-data-at-risk-increasing-chances-of-identity-theft/#60d78fcd5fdd

core tenet of most corporate boards, which is where we need the visibility to come from. There are also lots of examples where companies work with national and international law enforcement agencies to bring cybercriminals to justice. As you can imagine this can be challenging as laws and jurisdiction vary from country to country. But as we align around the importance of bringing cybercriminals to justice, we are seeing jurisdictional relations and data sharing across agencies improve. There are also threat sharing consortiums that ensure information about threats is widely available.

Additionally, initiatives like No More Ransom, which makes ransomware decryption keys freely available, have gone a long way toward helping consumers and businesses recover from cyberattacks. For the past couple of years ransomware has been a particularly nasty type of malware. "Ransomware is a type of malicious software from cryptovirology that threatens to publish the victim's data or perpetually block access to it unless a ransom is paid. While some simple ransomware may lock the system in a way which is not difficult for a knowledgeable person to reverse, more advanced malware uses a technique called cryptoviral extortion, in which it encrypts the victim's files, making them inaccessible, and demands a ransom payment to decrypt them."[107]

Finally, let's talk a little about how companies share data with third parties. I've made all kinds of statements comparing your data to cash; and they hold true. Legal and legitimate big businesses have grown by virtue of capitalizing upon or trading your data. It's a source of secondary revenue for some businesses, and it's a primary source for others.

Let's start with you as the source of secondary revenue for a company. A business (depending on if their terms and conditions allow for it) may collect, compile, and sell lists of their clients to others—that could be to another business who may want to reach you by adding you to their mailing list, or it could be to a major data broker that has those vats of data I mentioned before. What makes this data valuable is that there's a history attached to it. Your history.

---

[107] https://en.wikipedia.org/wiki/Ransomware

To the extent that this data is anonymized or not, it can present you as a highly qualified target audience for advertising a product or service.

As to what data as a secondary source of revenue looks like in practice, let's do a little sidestep and talk about your DNA.

Sit on the couch long enough or browse for a bit on the internet and you'll likely see various companies' ads for DNA kits. At a certain time of year, they'll position the kits as "a great gift for the holidays." The proposition is this: you'll get a low-cost DNA test that can tell you a great deal about your ancestry, including what region(s) of the world your family hails from and maybe even indicate your family's risk for certain diseases. The pitch works. In November 2018, one such DNA kit provider, Ancestry, claimed it broke its all-time sales record in advance of the gift-giving season.[108] If you find yourself interested in just how accurate these tests are, like how they go about pinpointing if your family is from Sicily or Crete and a number of other factoids that make for great dinner party conversation starters, there's plenty to read up on.

These companies are coming under increasing scrutiny as they increase in popularity. So, let's talk about why these companies offer these tests at such low cost. Your DNA winds up in a database. First, your data becomes yet another point that helps make their testing more accurate. Second, it allows companies like these to enter partnerships with others, such as the announced partnership between DNA kit provider 23andMe with a giant of the pharma industry, GlaxoSmithKline:

"… to potentially develop new drugs and treatments, which will include the sharing of anonymized, de-identified customer DNA. There's certainly a world of good that can be accomplished by further studying our genetics, and the company says it lets customers choose whether to share their data with GlaxoSmithKline or for future research purposes (if you decide your mind later, though, you're out

---

[108] https://www.ancestry.com/corporate/newsroom/press-releases/ancestry-breaks-november-sales-record

of luck). But it might leave a sour taste in your mouth to know that you'll never see a penny of the profits your DNA helped make possible…"[109]

Sure, this example may come across as a little extreme because it shows how a company can make money from your DNA rather than from the IP address of your smartphone whenever you access the internet. Yet the business model remains the same. You offer something personal, you get something free or low-cost from a company in return, and the company makes money on the back end by using what you've provided for any number of purposes. And, per the terms and conditions, you have no control over the exact nature or goal of those purposes.

One other point of consideration with these at-home genetic testing companies is that they have, in some cases, shared their DNA databases with law enforcement. I think we can agree that bringing rapists, murderers, and other major criminals to justice is a good thing; however, at issue is whether or not the company actually discloses any such voluntary sharing with law enforcement. Such was the case in February 2019 when, as reported in the *New York Times*, FamilyTreeDNA revealed to its users that the company indeed opened up its database of roughly two million records to the FBI a year earlier.[110]

According to the *New York Times* article, "FamilyTreeDNA had marketed itself as a leader of consumer privacy and a fierce protector of user data, refusing, unlike some of its competitors, to sell information to third parties … setting off a backlash among its loyal users who felt betrayed and igniting another debate over privacy and ethical issues with investigators using genealogical sites to solve crimes." Certainly, events such as this prompt numerous discussions regarding the balance between personal privacy and the safety of our broader communities. They also remind us that once our personal information digitally passes hands to another party, there's a good

---

[109] https://gizmodo.com/dont-take-the-dna-test-youll-probably-get-for-christmas-1831068871
[110] https://www.nytimes.com/2019/02/04/business/family-tree-dna-fbi.html

chance we've lost control of it and have little to no say (or knowledge) of how it gets used.

If you signed up for one of these services in the past and now find yourself having second thoughts, an article published by the nonprofit Consumer Reports (CR) outlines the steps you can take to have your DNA removed from three of the largest providers: 23andMe, Ancestry, and MyHeritage. Keep in mind that terms and conditions can change over time, along with the web pages that allow you to revoke your permissions, have your test sample destroyed, or exercise other privacy-minded options. At the time I'm writing this, the big three providers maintain comprehensive privacy policies that you can view online and offer ways to remove data that hasn't been used in research. The CR article notes something else: 40 of the 90 companies researched in the article did not post a privacy policy regarding genetic data.[111] In the event that you (or someone you know) have used an in-home genetic testing service of any kind, it's definitely worth your time to read the full article.

As we shift from DNA back to the digital world, there are many companies that make customer data a primary source of income, and some of them are worth in the billions of U.S. dollars. These are the data brokers and direct marketing organizations that maintain those vats of customer data. Names like Acxiom, Epsilon, and Merkle fill out the field. No worries if you haven't heard of them. They're used by researchers and marketers who look to identify, target, and reach well-defined audiences. How do those audiences get defined so well? Data. These organizations further provide their own tools for insightful analysis of that data. Sometimes they also offer their own platforms and partnerships for getting messages in front of people online.

These practices have been going on for years, yet you can easily imagine how computers, the internet, and now mobile devices with GPS location tracking have created batches of data that are richer than ever before and have rightfully prompted all manner of ethical questions. In a nutshell, how much data is too much—especially

---

[111] https://www.consumerreports.org/health-privacy/how-to-delete-genetic-data-from-23andme-ancestry-other-sites/

when it's in the hands of a private, for-profit enterprise that often collects it from people who aren't fully aware it's being collected and what it's being used for?

Again, if this practice takes place above board, with all parties being aware and consenting to it as part of an understood "value exchange," it's fine. It's a transaction between willing parties—I give you this, you give me that in return. As for these vats of data themselves, the idea is that you, as a consumer, should see some benefits out of them too. Many companies view this access to insights as a way to better align their business around the real needs of people, in ways that go far beyond serving up better ads. With these insights, they reshape their customer service, the way they design their products, the way they structure their business, and even the way they lay out the interior of their brick-and-mortar stores— all in an effort to create a better experience for you. As with any tool, how companies affect you as they use data from these data brokers and direct marketing organizations depends on how they choose to wield it. Put plainly, companies can indeed use consumer data for "good," and many of them do just that.

Of course, where the concern comes in is through your awareness and consent. If you don't want to participate, you shouldn't. Here in the U.S. that can introduce complications. You may not know that a company shares data with third parties, in what fashion, and, specifically, with whom for what end. Some apps and services allow you to "opt out" and not participate in such sharing, whether absolutely or by degrees of participation, while still allowing you access to them. Others, it's all or nothing: if you don't want your data shared, you don't get to use the service. Again, we call up the GDPR, which is intended to help you get a better grasp on what a company is or is not doing and whether you want to take part in it all.

In some instances, the industry has your back. Above and beyond legislation, a number of tech leaders and CEOs have taken a strong philosophical stance on data privacy, notably Tim Cook of Apple. In a March 2018 interview, he was prompted on the topic of security and bluntly responded:

"We've never believed that these detailed profiles of people, that have incredibly deep personal information that is patched together from several sources, should exist," Cook said. Later, he added that those detailed profiles of consumers "can be abused against our democracy. It can be abused by advertisers as well."[112]

Zip ahead from there to October of the same year when Apple levied an all-new requirement on apps that are submitted to its App Store. Each new or updated app must include a link to the app developer's privacy policy that explains:

- What data the app/service collects.
- How this data is collected.
- What is done with that data.
- How data is stored.
- How users can revoke consent and demand deletion of their data.
- Further, the policy must also promise that any third party that the app developer shares data with must also provide the same disclosures.[113]

This should look quite familiar because it mirrors aspects of the GDPR regulation. Tim Cook has gone on record stating that he's "not a fan" of regulation, rather that he prefers self-regulation by the industry itself. To Apple's credit, it has a great reputation for consumer privacy which is reflected in a cultlike following and the ability to charge a premium for its branded goods and services. A couple of years ago, McAfee surveyed 2,700 consumers and asked which well-known companies did the best job at protecting their private information. The companies named went beyond technology companies to include consumer goods companies. It should come as no surprise that Apple led the list, with 25% saying they trusted Apple to keep their private information private. Also, in 2019, for an

---

[112] https://www.theverge.com/2018/3/28/17172718/apple-ceo-tim-cook-privacy-facebook-cambridge-analytica
[113] https://blogs.computerworld.com/article/3302380/mobile-wireless/apple-insists-developers-ramp-up-their-privacy-commitments.html

unprecedented 12th year in a row, *Fortune* awarded Apple its "Most Admired"[114] company designation. Certainly, there are a lot of factors that go into that designation, but I'm confident that Apple's stance on customer privacy was a meaningful component.

I predict we will see plenty of push and pull from legislators and industry as they look to solve for this issue of data privacy. Complicating that tug-of-war will be dollars (as you likely guessed). Big data is big business. And with artificial intelligence able to sift through the mountains of data to quickly glean useful insights, big data equates to mining for gold. Major data brokers and tech players that built their business models on data collection will make interesting headlines as they navigate the coming years and adjust to a world where more and more consumers and their representatives demand improvements in data privacy. We live in quite a time.

What to do about all this? As one person, one family, you can feel quite small compared to the governments, tech giants, and data brokers who hold sway over data collection practices and regulations. We've talked plenty about this environment, along with the data we create within it. Now, let's talk solutions.

Enter the Family CIO

I took a quick count and totaled 37 connected things in my home. That number goes up every year, and my data lake has likely reflected that influx of devices. Think about it, though. Remember when we had just one device, our clunky desktop computer, that connected to the internet? Remember when it seemed like a big deal that we had like three devices that connected to the internet? With this growing presence of connected devices in our homes (and hey, we're plenty happy to have many of them) comes the care and effort it takes to manage them—actually, the care and effort we *need* to put into managing them. Plenty of us don't manage the thriving network of computers, phones, game consoles, and smart devices that are now everyday household fixtures, and this is where plenty of security and privacy issues can rush in.

---

[114] https://www.cultofmac.com/601994/apple-is-most-admired-company-for-record-12th-year-in-a-row/

There is someone who can take care of all that, though.

Let me introduce you to the family chief information officer, or family CIO. It's you. It's your partner too. As the adults in your home, you're in charge, which includes ensuring that your digital home is just as safe as the rest of your physical home. That covers your network, your devices, how they're used, who's using them, their security, the security of your data—all of that. You are indeed a CIO.

Just as a business CIO has tools to make his or her job easier, so do you. Consumer security has caught up to, and in plenty of cases anticipated, the needs of today's super-connected household. You can find all manner of products that will streamline security and take some of the headache out of it. I'll start off with a quick list of things you can do, and then follow up with further detail on each item.

The Family CIO Checklist
Making Your Digital World More Private and Secure

- Pause.
- Use password managers to create highly secure passwords for all of your accounts.
- Avoid saving passwords and credit card information online.
- Use encryption whenever you can.
- Back up your data.
- Consider protecting your entire home network at the point of internet entry: your router.
- Consider using a virtual private network (VPN) for connecting to the internet.
- Act on notices of breaches and threats.
- Conduct regular "App Audits" of the apps you have on your devices.
- Educate your family on good behaviors and set expectations for how the internet is used in your home.
- Use comprehensive security software to protect your devices.

Pause. Yes, pause. One of the keys to reducing your likelihood of being a victim is to stop and think before clicking on that email link or SMS message. Ninety-one percent of all cyberattacks start with phishing email.[115] As a reminder, "phishing is the fraudulent attempt to obtain sensitive information such as usernames, passwords and credit card details by disguising as a trustworthy entity in an electronic communication. Typically carried out by email spoofing or instant messaging, it often directs users to enter personal information at a fake website, the look and feel of which are identical to the legitimate site."[116] Before blindly clicking on the link in an email ask yourself, was I expecting an email from this person or company. I've gotten to the point where even if the email is legit, I still avoid clicking on links in the email. For example, every month I get an email from my bank telling me my statement is ready and they provide a link to the statement. Instead of clicking on the link in the email I go to my bank's website and log in to check my statement.

Use password managers to create complex passwords for all of your accounts. Some security software offers this as part of the base package, yet you can get this separately too if it isn't in yours or you prefer something else. I've talked a lot about using strong, unique passwords as a line of defense. A top-rated password manager will create them for you, plus do the work of remembering them so you can log into your apps and accounts easily and more securely than before. They can also automate changing your passwords on a regular basis, which is a great security habit to get into.

Avoid saving passwords and credit card information online. While most browsers over the years have improved how they handle sensitive information like passwords and credit cards, they are still inherently risky. When saving passwords, the biggest reason you are much better off using a password manager than your browser is that most password managers run on a variety of platforms, so you're very likely to use your password manager on all your computers, smartphones, and tablets. If you want to facilitate future payments

---

[115] https://www.darkreading.com/endpoint/91--of-cyberattacks-start-with-a-phishing-email/d/d-id/1327704
[116] https://en.wikipedia.org/wiki/Phishing

to your favorite online store, you should consider using something like PayPal. In the event that PayPal ever experiences a breach of your credit card, you only need to change it with them instead of trying to recall all the online stores you may have used your credit card on.

Use encryption whenever possible. If you're not familiar with encryption, according to Wikipedia, "it is the process of encoding a message or information in such a way that only authorized parties can access it and those who are not authorized cannot."[117] In other words, encryption protects your data and communications from prying eyes. For most of us there are two areas when we should routinely use encryption. First, you should encrypt any device that allows it, especially your smartphone. If someone was to steal or get unauthorized access to your smartphone and it's not encrypted, then all they have to do is connect it via a USB cable to a computer to see all the information on it. Second, you should always make sure that any website you go to uses encrypted communications. The easiest way to determine whether a website uses encrypted communications is by looking at your URL and seeing https:// before the location you are going to. The good news is that most websites use encrypted communications today. If you come across a website that does not have encryption, do not share any type of credentials or other personal information about yourself as that information will be sent in such a way that could be easily stolen. Finally, when considering a cloud storage provider or purchasing a new connected thing in your home, part of your buying decision should be whether or not they use encryption for your data at rest and in motion.

Back up your data. Today's computer manufacturers and application services make this much easier to do than it was before. When purchasing a new computer, whether a PC or a Mac, the operating system typically offers a cloud storage service right out of the box. For PCs, it's Microsoft OneDrive, and for Mac, it's iCloud. As far as third parties go, Dropbox is a popular option for cloud storage, as are Mozy and Carbonite. All of these services offer plans, typically based on how much storage you need, yet the good news is that cloud storage is a relatively cheap commodity these days. Just a

---

[117] https://en.wikipedia.org/wiki/Encryption

few bucks invested in one can save you major heartburn, or outright heartbreak, down the pike.

The way this works is that you have a folder that not only stores your files locally on your computer but with a cloud service as well, like OneDrive, iCloud, or Dropbox. Because these files are stored elsewhere on a cloud server via the internet, you can access them from any number of different devices, such as your laptop or phone. Likewise, that also means your files are backed up. Should your computer fail, become compromised, or fall victim to a morning coffee incident that takes out your keyboard, you can still access your files from another computer (perhaps a new one). Also, going with a cloud storage provider makes transferring files onto a new computer you purchase a lickety-split affair. Just access the cloud service on your new computer and start downloading away.

Another means of backing up your data is rather old school, yet it provides an additional layer of security and redundancy for you. Hop online or pop into your local retailer and pick up a portable hard drive. These drives plug right into your computer with a cable, and with them you can copy all of your folders onto that drive. Once you're done, you can stash it away in a safe spot. By going this route, you have a local copy of all your files on a separate hard drive, ready for use should disaster strike. The drawback to this method is that you have to be diligent. The files are only as current as how often you back them up. It's a little extra work, but the peace of mind is well worth it. After all, imagine what life would be like if you lost all of your data—files, photos, emails, and so forth. If you have a sick feeling in the pit of your stomach at the thought, you'll know why this is so important.

An additional step you should take to protect yourself is to back up the image of your computer. Think of an image as a comprehensive capture your data settings and computer configuration. So, if your drive crashes, you can replace the faulty drive, access your image, and then restore your system back to where it was the last time the image was taken. Images are also useful for when an update or other activity makes your computer a bit unstable. In such cases, you can restore your computer to an earlier image before that update or activity took place (i.e., back when it was still stable). Note that this is different than backing up your files and photos and email. Images are a failsafe for your computer, not your individual files.

Windows PCs have backup utilities that can create these images, as do Macs by way of the Time Machine application that's included with the Mac operating system (macOS). As you can probably tell, you'll want to create and save these images on a separate drive where they'll be safe—and ready in the event your computer dies a hard death and needs a new drive. Again, you can use an external drive for this purpose. Just be mindful to do this on a regular basis. I suggest every month. Also, keep the previous month's image on your drive as well. As with all things under this topic, redundancy is your pal!

Consider protecting your entire home network at the point of internet entry: your router. Once more, I'll bring up the advice I passed along in chapter 1. Router manufacturers like ARRIS and D-Link now offer internet routers that protect all of the devices that connect to them—things with and without a screen—including smart thermostats, camera systems, your voice assistants, and everything else. Via a smartphone app, you can institute settings that block suspicious connections, establish parental controls, and more, plus you can shut down your internet access with a tap. Increasingly, this kind of "blanket protection" is becoming a must. I encourage you to look into it.

Consider using a virtual private network (VPN) for connecting to the internet. Companies have used VPNs for decades now to protect their employees and their data from prying eyes. I'll skip the technical details as to how they work, but a fine way of thinking about it is this: a VPN creates an encrypted private connection that secures your activities and transactions. As for the privacy issues I talked about earlier in this chapter, a VPN is a fantastic tool for protecting your privacy. In effect, it makes your online activities anonymous. You'll find numerous options for different VPN providers with a search online, all with different pricing structures and costs. I will caution you to research your choice carefully, as there are some shadowy players out there, so look to reviews from reputable online technology publications like *CNET* or *PCMag* for their opinions of the best options. Also, be sure to carefully read the license agreements to determine which VPN apps create logs of your activities and which don't. You can decide what is best for you, but you should understand what the app developer is capturing.

Act on notices of breaches and threats. A big part of the family CIO's job is to jump in and react as needed to fix a problem. That could take the form of your kid asking you to troubleshoot a bad internet connection on their tablet, but it can also entail anything from viruses to spam to phishing emails that try and trick you into giving your information by masquerading as a legitimate business or individual. Needless to say, this is a big list of stuff that a family CIO may have to worry about. Happily, if you have security software in place, you have a big helping hand. It will notify you in many instances when something on your device or in your network requires your attention. Plus, it will typically offer you a solution to remedy whatever is wrong.

Another bonus is that security software can come with live support from the company that produces it. In all, as the family CIO, you don't need to know *everything* about technology to run the network. In fact, every good CIO has a staff, so think of the technical support that comes with your security software as experts you can turn to. You can also look into any number of the reputable "tech concierge" services that offer consultative and preventative services in addition to "break-fix" support when you need it.

You'll want to jump in and react as soon as possible when news breaks of a data breach at a major retailer, insurance company, hotel chain, or any other business or organization. You may read about it when you're online, or you may receive a notice from the company that's been affected by the breach indicating that your data could be at risk. Either way, you can take the following immediate actions:

- **Change your password.** Most people will rotate between the same two to three passwords for all of their personal accounts. While this makes it easier to remember your credentials, it also makes it easier for hackers to access more than one of your accounts. Use a unique password for every one of your accounts and, as mentioned earlier in the list, employ a password manager to make changing and managing your passwords simple and effective.

- **Place a fraud alert.** If you suspect that your data might have been compromised, place a fraud alert on your credit. This not only ensures that any new or recent credit requests undergo scrutiny but also allows you to have extra copies of your credit report so you can check for suspicious activity.
- **Freeze your credit.** Freezing your credit will make it impossible for criminals to take out loans or open up new accounts in your name. To do this effectively, you will need to freeze your credit at each of the three major credit reporting agencies (Equifax, TransUnion, and Experian).
- **Consider using identity theft protection.** Besides helping you monitor your accounts, it will alert you of any suspicious activity and help you to regain any losses in case something goes wrong. Some even include monitoring the dark web (where hackers buy and sell personal information) for any activity tied to your email, Social Security number, credit cards, etc., and will then alert you should activity be detected. Again, you'll want to check expert reviews to research which package will work best for your household.
- **Update your privacy settings.** Be careful with how much of your personal information you share online. Make sure your social media accounts and mobile apps are on private and use multi-factor authentication to help protect your accounts from being hacked.
- **Be vigilant about checking your accounts.** If you suspect that your personal data has been compromised, frequently check your bank account and credit activity. This will help you stop fraudulent activity in its tracks. I do this daily. It only takes a couple of minutes and I can quickly scan my top bank accounts to determine if anything unusual has taken place. Also, many banks and credit card companies offer free alerts that notify you via email or text messages when new purchases are made, if there's an unusual charge, or when your account balance drops to a certain level.

Conduct regular "App Audits" of the apps you have on your devices. Another way you can pour less data into your lake is to throttle your output by reducing the number of apps you use. What's more, fewer apps can mean fewer avenues of attack a hacker or fraudster can take. This is actually a fun little exercise. Start by unlocking your phone and looking at all of the apps you have installed. Next, take stock of all of them. How many of them are apps you actually use on a regular basis, if at all anymore? Then make some decisions—and start deleting.

Some apps you can delete quite simply, like old games or utilities you haven't tapped into for months. Other apps will have an account associated with them, so you'll need to go in and shut down the associated account to really delete them. I usually do this about once per month with an eye toward removing apps. I typically find 2-3 apps to remove that I either don't use often enough or don't view as meaningful.

At this point, you'll have more space on your phone and a less cluttered screen as well. You may even find that you get more time out of your battery. Now, with the apps that remain, you can do some homework. Find out what you can about the data policies and practices of these apps. And remember, if you're an iPhone user, the App Store has that new disclosure policy I talked about. Just visit the app's landing page in the App Store and get your info there.

This is also a good time to update all your apps if you haven't already. Keeping your apps current protects you from attacks and intrusions as well. When it comes to updating my apps, this is another thing I do on a daily basis. Not only do I get the latest capabilities, but I know that those updates normally include security fixes.

Another part of your audit is going in and looking at what permissions you've given your apps. Many app developers will ask for access to things like your location, browsing history, and even your contacts, all by default. If you have a gaming or flashlight app that asks for these things, that's a red flag. Deny those permissions, or just trash the app. There's no reason a game or flashlight should need these things. In most cases you can find a similar app that doesn't have onerous permissions.

Yes, an app audit can mean a fair share of work. Just take it in blocks. It's a strong measure that's worth the effort if you're concerned about your privacy, what data you're sharing, and what data you're pouring into your lake.

Educate your family on good behaviors and set expectations for how the internet is used in your home. Another way a CIO runs a tight ship is to set policies for the organization—rules about what devices are allowed on the network, what sites they can access, who can use them, and many, many more policies for keeping people and their data secure. As the family CIO, you get to do the same. (My hope is that your reading of the first chapters of the book has helped you formulate a strong point of view on what those rules are for you and your family.)

Although you're in charge, you needn't impose these policies from up on high. You can bring them forward as a conversation, simply letting your kids know what the rules and expectations for the internet are, just like any other rules you set forth. Of course, how you go about setting rules is all up to your situation and parenting style. However, when you make changes, communicate them first and be clear about why you've tightened (or relaxed!) any rules you'll put in place.

Use comprehensive security software to protect your devices. This is an easy one, and it repeats my earlier advice about getting this in place for your entire household. Today's security software is much more than the good old antivirus software you've probably been using for years. It can protect multiple PCs, Macs, smartphones, and tablets with one subscription that can cover your whole family, even if they are not living at home all the time. They also go beyond basic antivirus protection by looking after your privacy while guarding against identity theft and much more, including browser protection that keeps you from clicking on links to shady websites.

Dispose of (Tech) Properly

We keep plenty of information about our lives and livelihoods on our computers, phones, and tablets, so when it's time to upgrade one of those devices it's also time to get rid of your old tech properly. This brings up a couple of notions…

The first is the issue of electronic waste. The tech we love contains lead, flame retardants, mercury, and cadmium—all stuff that, if not disposed of properly, has dramatic impacts on things such as our drinking water and air quality (when burned in garbage incinerators). Plus, our gadgets are packed with all sorts of valuable materials that can be reused. For example, according to the U.S. Environmental Protection Agency:

- *Recycling one million laptops saves the energy equivalent to the electricity used by more than 3,500 US homes in a year.*

- *For every million cell phones we recycle, 35 thousand pounds of copper, 772 pounds of silver, 75 pounds of gold and 33 pounds of palladium can be recovered.*[118]

Accordingly, major cell phone carriers have buyback programs, and plenty of communities have rules and dedicated locations for the disposal of electronic waste. Moreover, a quick search online will turn up plenty of electronic waste disposal companies and a number of options where you can donate your old gear or even sell it back for a few bucks.

The second notion is security. The hard drive in that old laptop likely has your tax info and bank records on it. Your phone is absolutely jam-packed with details about your life, including your emails, your contact lists, and a transcription of all the texts you've sent. You'll want to wipe these devices clean. With computers and laptops, operating systems have utilities that can securely erase a drive by writing random (nonsense) data on them. Or, if you want to be really sure, you can remove the hard drive, put on some safety glasses, and drill a hole through it. (Not that many of us will do this,

---

[118] https://www.epa.gov/recycle/electronics-donation-and-recycling

but brute force that dismantles a drive is an almost certain way to ensure that data will not see the light of day again.)

Probably the most popular device that's destined to be either given away or disposed of is your old smartphone. You know, the device with a battery life measured in minutes instead of hours and a fancy spider-webbed display thanks to that drop in the Safeway parking lot. Both major smartphone operating systems (iOS and Android) have common steps for preparing the device for someone else or disposal. Those steps include:

1. Before starting, make sure the device is fully charged or connected to a power source. Ideally, you should have it connected to a power source since the battery is most likely on its last legs. This is important because some of the steps may take a long time and the last thing you'll want is to lose power halfway through the process.

2. Back up the device and all the apps you plan on using going forward. Doing this will make sure you have everything you need when you bring your new smartphone online. This is super important because once you wipe the device you will no longer have access to anything that was stored on it. I mention backing up the data from your regularly used apps separately because some data from apps won't be backed up when you create a backup of the device. For example, WhatsApp has its own backup system, so backing up your device will not include your WhatsApp messages.

3. Once you have all your data backed up, you'll want to remove accounts from your smartphone. You most likely have email accounts or ways to access things like app stores. Go into your system settings to remove any of those accounts. How to do this varies a bit by operating system and which version of the operating system you have.

4. After everything is backed up and you've removed your accounts, it's time to wipe the device. Like removing your accounts, this varies between operating systems and which version you have, but you will go into the system settings and look for General on iOS and General management on your Android. There you will find options to reset the device to the factory default.

5. If you have an SD card for additional storage, be sure to remove it and either put it into your new smartphone or get an SD card reader and use your computer to copy and move the data stored on SD card to your new smartphone.

There are lots of good articles online about how to properly wipe your smartphone before selling or discarding it. Be sure to specify the operating system and version level when conducting your search. In particular, I found a CNET article about it to be very well structured and informative.[119]

In all, we can't simply toss our old tech stuff in the dustbin when it hits the end of its useful life span for us. Make sure you wipe your personal information from the device. Then you can choose to dispose of it at an electronic waste facility, turn it in to a recycler, or see if it's worth donating or if you can claim a little cash back from it through resale or a buyback program.

So, You Want to Erase Your Presence on the Internet

Considering ways to delete yourself from the internet is a common theme at this stage in your life. We wake up one day and realize that we've way overexposed ourselves online. While it's impossible to ensure the complete removal of your digital existence, there are some steps you can take to ebb the flow of information into your data lake. Chandra Steele wrote an excellent article on this very subject for *PCMag*.[120] It's worthwhile reading as it outlines ways to delete your social media accounts and has further advice about keeping a low profile.

One interesting thing Steele points out is that the average person has about 130 active accounts per email address. These could be accounts associated with online forums that you belong to, ecommerce sites, and maybe a few businesses that have you on their mailing list. Go ahead and remove yourself from them. It's relatively

---

[119] https://www.cnet.com/how-to/how-to-wipe-your-phone-or-tablet-before-selling/
[120] https://www.pcmag.com/news/366026/what-to-do-when-you-want-to-delete-yourself-from-the-interne

easy to do, as those emails almost always have an "unsubscribe" link at the bottom. So cast a critical eye on those newsletters and emails that pop into your inbox. If you don't absolutely need them in your life, unsubscribe.

What Steele's article outlines is a great start. However, if you want to take it to the next level, consider taking a look at the fourth edition of *Hiding from the Internet: Eliminating Personal Online Information*, by Michael Bazzell. IntelTechniques.com has a public forum and regularly scans the hard-to-find places on the internet to identify new opt-out techniques for various services. This latest edition of their book explains how you can do the following:

- Remove your personal information from public databases and people search websites.
- Create free anonymous mail addresses, email addresses, and telephone numbers.
- Control your privacy settings on social networks and remove sensitive data.
- Provide disinformation to conceal true private details.
- Apply proper security to your computers using free resources.
- Force data brokers to stop sharing your information with private and public organizations.
- Prevent marketing companies from monitoring your browsing and shopping habits.
- Remove your landline and cellular telephone numbers from online websites.
- Use a credit freeze to eliminate the worry of financial identity theft and fraud.
- Change your future habits to promote complete privacy and anonymity.
- Conduct a complete background check to verify proper information removal.
- Purchase a home or vehicle anonymously.

- Install a proper home firewall with absolute VPN kill-switch.[121]

That should cover pretty much everything needed to remove yourself from the internet and then some. The key, as Steele points out, is to then stay off the grid, which would include avoiding social media sites, browsing privately, shopping locally (not online), and switching off your phone's GPS to prevent apps from tracking your whereabouts. In fact, she suggests ditching your smartphone entirely and going with a low-tech mobile phone instead.

Your Personal Information Is Not Always Required

One of the privacy and identity challenges I find super interesting is how often certain businesses ask for personal information such as your Social Security number or date of birth when it's actually not required. You should always be very leery of providing personal information such as your Social Security number, date of birth, or other personal identifiers unless it's absolutely required. This holds true for both online and offline activities. According to NBC's Herb Weisbaum:

There are certain times when Social Security numbers must be used. This is not a complete list, but here are some of the major situations when they are required:

- *Most major financial transactions (such as buying a new home or car)*
- *Employment records*
- *Tax returns (federal and state)*
- *Medicare benefits*
- *Contact with the Social Security Administration*
- *Applications for a hunting, fishing or other recreational license.*

Some states have their own requirements for providing Social Security numbers. For instance, in Washington you must list your Social Security number the first time you apply for a driver's license. Federal law (The Intelligence Reform

---

[121] https://inteltechniques.com/book2.html

and Terrorism Prevention Act of 2004) prohibits states from displaying your Social Security number on your license or vehicle registration forms, but they can still collect this information.

Because the Social Security number has become a personal identifier, you will need to use it for many other transactions -- basically anything that involves a credit check or background check. A potential landlord or prospective employer will probably request it. And anyone lending you money or extending credit will need it.[122]

We often see medical providers ask for your Social Security number. They typically want it in the event they can't collect payment from you, but it's not required. My point is, don't just provide personally identifiable information about yourself because someone or some organization asked for it. When in doubt, ask the organization why they are collecting it and determine if you are legally bound to provide it. Another consideration is to determine if the information they are asking for is required to deliver the service. For example, if you purchased a new fitness tracker, providing your date of birth might provide a more customized experience. Conversely, if you're prompted by a company to fill in your birthday before downloading a research paper it is likely not required.

We Can't Ignore the Problem (Security Fatigue vs. Optimism Bias)

In addition to thinking about ways we can remove our presence online; this is also the time where many of us start to suffer from security fatigue or optimism bias. They are slightly different. Security fatigue comes from us throwing our arms up in surrender to the non-stop bombardment of security news and choosing to do nothing because the bad guys are going to get to us anyway, whereas optimism bias is the belief that something bad will happen to someone else and not us. In all, that leaves many Americans doing little, if anything, to protect themselves.

---

[122] http://www.nbcnews.com/id/12359845/ns/business-consumer_news/t/when-are-social-security-numbers-required/#.XFwp8c9Kgl4

According to a recently released report from ERP Maestro that examined the relationship Americans have with cybercrime and identity theft, 76% of Americans believe it is inevitable that they will fall victim to either identity theft or some form of cybercrime. As a result, 48% confess that they are not concerned about becoming a victim. The report found that when it comes to consumer attitudes and behaviors, 57% of Americans believe that if something happens, the damage will be reversed."[123]

Both security fatigue and optimism bias need to be kept in check. I get it. We often feel helpless in a world where the dark forces seem to muster more energy than we can handle, and the tide of breaches and other security news can feel overwhelming. Since I live in a security-rich world by way of my profession, I make it a point to balance the news that I receive about what's going on in the space with good news. It helps me to keep a positive outlook on the world in general. I also practice what I preach in that the tips and insights I'm sharing throughout this book are part of my regular routines. If you do the same, I am confident that you will neither suffer from security fatigue nor indulge in optimism bias, and you will be able to enjoy your digital journey.

What Did We Learn?

Security and privacy are major issues of our day and age, and they're only getting thornier as we welcome more and more devices into our home that collect all manner of data and information about who we are, what we're doing, and where we're going. Forces in the public and private sectors are both looking to address it, and meanwhile we can feel a little caught in the middle. However, with effort (and, for the moment, a lot of it) we can take an increasing degree of control by limiting the places where we share our data and making an informed choice about any potential tradeoffs when we do. We'll never stop the flow of data into our data lakes, but we can take steps to ensure we feel more comfortable about what's flowing in and know (most) of it will be used in ways that benefit us in some

---

[123] https://www.infosecurity-magazine.com/news/americans-feel-fated-to-fall-prey/

way or other. Data is a reality of modern life. It absolutely has its benefits, and we can stem its flow.

This is one of those chapters you may need to read a couple of times as you settle into your role as the family CIO. Your position as the family CIO may scare some of you, whereas others will find it empowering. Regardless of how you feel about this distinction, it's on you to take the necessary steps to safeguard yourself and your loved ones. There are plenty of resources that you can lean on to stay informed of what's happening in the space. I stay current by using news aggregators like Flipboard to keep me up to date on the several topics that canvass the cybersecurity and privacy space. My filters cover a broad spectrum of topics that either directly or indirectly impact this ever-expanding space. If that feels a bit daunting, you may want to consider following me on Twitter @GaryJDavis or subscribing to McAfee Securing Tomorrow Blogs to read highly informative posts about what you can do to stay safe in an increasingly risky online and connected world.

7

AGES 55 AND UP – EMPTY NESTERS AND SILVER SURFERS

As we age, we may think that the number of connected devices in our home will have been pared down, particularly after the kids fly the coop and take their clutch of digital devices with them. However, given the way technology (and the marketplace) is going, that's not the case at all. Even for empty nesters, it's all too easy to accumulate more and more "things" that are connected to the internet. When you stroll through a home improvement or appliance store, you'll see connected screens on refrigerators and Wi-Fi enabled stoves that you can control from your home assistant or smartphone. Plenty of other appliances and household fixtures now get the connected treatment: thermostats, vacuum cleaners, door locks, and security camera systems pair up with the internet and allow you to program and control them online as well. "Modern convenience" now means "connected," and what was once a novelty is now the norm: we have more connected devices than we could have imagined just a few short years ago because connectivity has now become a standard feature in products—and not just in the high-end models. Every time I visit my mom, she talks about a new smart TV or other connected thing she has in her house. I think it's awesome that she is so comfortable with all this new technology.

Although, honestly, I often cringe when I consider the security and privacy challenges she may not be taking into consideration.

Some of these newly connected devices make great sense to me. For example, being able to remotely manage my thermostats not only offers me great convenience but also allows me to keep my energy bill in check. Admittedly, some connected things make me scratch my head: I don't think I need a smart toothbrush to remind me to brush for two minutes and make sure I get every part of my mouth. But who am I to question where innovations like those may take us? I just know that I'm enjoying the journey. As I mentioned in the previous chapter, I have 37 connected things in my home today. Every year that number grows, and I genuinely don't see an end in sight as I constantly look for those devices that will allow me to enjoy my life in ways I can't even comprehend right now.

As first mentioned in chapter 3, this growing connectivity is the phenomenon called the internet of things (IoT), a phrase used to describe the massive amounts of connected devices on the internet (in addition to computers, smartphones, and tablets), some 23 billion of them in 2018.[124]

As we all face this next evolution of the internet and are learning how these devices can benefit our lives and homes, it is becoming increasingly important for us to understand the security and privacy issues associated with them. That way, we not only can select the best IoT devices for our lifestyle but also implement the proper security and privacy protections for them. At the same time, we must be aware and weigh the value of these conveniences against the knowledge that they will pump an entirely new class of data into our data lake—captured from how we go about our day.

And there's no doubt that many IoT devices are fantastic conveniences. Some of the ways companies will pitch these devices to us will focus on energy savings, time savings, and money savings—and sometimes even sanity savings. We're busy, time-pressed people with plenty of things we'd rather be doing than

[124] https://www.statista.com/statistics/471264/iot-number-of-connected-devices-worldwide/

spending an hour vacuuming the house. IoT devices, by design, give us some of that time back, à la George Jetson in his space-age automated home above the clouds.

Thanks to the IoT, you can run your connected vacuum cleaner remotely, on demand, right from your phone. You can use IoT devices to turn your lights on and off, water your lawn with a connected sprinkler system, set your thermostats, unlock your doors, open the garage, just to name a few of the more popular applications. They also promise an increased sense of security, like doorbell systems that alert you as to who is at the door via a remote camera, even when you're not at home. Or how about this—want to check in on your pup during the day while you're out? You can buy a remote pet sitter that rolls around your home and lets you see and speak to your dog via an app. And if puppy looks a little peckish, you can even dispense a treat remotely too. How fun is that?

Home assistants are another breed of IoT device that have absolutely exploded onto the scene in recent years, with well over 200 million of them sold by Amazon and Google as of early 2019 according to reports from their manufacturers. If you don't have a home assistant, you've probably seen one, at least on a commercial that shows it being summoned with a "wake word" or "hot word" (like, "Hey, Google!") and then the device listens for various requests to fulfill.

A few request examples would be to conduct a search on the internet, call up music to play on your Bluetooth-connected speakers, get recipes, make hands-free calls, record a voice memo, tell your kids a story, or even tell a joke (although truthfully I have not heard a joke that would get a laugh in an old Borscht Belt comedy club, but that could just be me). To the extent that you want to knit your assistant into the operations of your household as sort of a master control, you can also connect it to your lights, your appliances, your thermostat—many of those devices I mentioned earlier.

Managing Your World of Connected Things

After reading up to this point (the previous chapter in particular), you know that all this digital convenience is generating a lot of data—personal data about you, your home, your routine, what you buy, and so forth. And if you're using a home assistant, the data generation is even more interesting from a privacy perspective: you're channeling all of this activity through one device made by one manufacturer who, in effect, has a direct connection into your kitchen, living room, or bedroom—wherever you have it set up. That's plenty to trust *anyone* with, let alone one company.

But here's where I can dampen, at least to some degree, any alarms that may be going off in your head. Although these devices do need to listen all the time in order to respond to the wake word, privacy policies posted by both Google and Amazon (two of the leading manufacturers of home assistants) say they only process words just before and following the wake word. According to a May 2018 article published by Techworld:

Google is clear that it does not record any ambient conversations around the Home device. The official data security and privacy support page states: "No. Google Home listens in short (a few seconds) snippets for the hotword. Those snippets are deleted if the hotword is not detected, and none of that information leaves your device until the hotword is heard.

"When Google Home detects that you've said, "OK Google," the LEDs on top of the device light up to tell you that recording is happening, Google Home records what you say, and sends that recording (including the few-second hotword recording) to Google in order to fulfill your request. You can delete those recordings through My Activity anytime."

Amazon is similarly clear in its Alexa and Alexa Device FAQ: "Amazon Echo and Echo Dot use on-device keyword spotting to detect the wake word. When these devices detect the wake word, they stream audio to the Cloud, including a fraction of a second of audio before the wake word."

You can also review voice interactions by visiting the history section in the settings of the Alexa App or the settings in the Google Home app. Users can even listen to audio sent to the cloud, delete voice clips and enter feedback.[125]

Of course, where there's data there's a possibility of that data getting out into the broader world, whether through an intentional hack, a fault in code, or a user error. In the months after these assistants hit the market came a series of news stories about conversations getting inadvertently recorded and sent to people on the owner's contact list,[126] people requesting information about themselves that their devices have collected about them only to get someone else's data instead,[127] and plenty of hyped-up clickbait articles warning people that "Big Brother" is listening in to them. In my own case, I recall a couple of months ago when I was talking to someone in my kitchen. The next thing I know one of my digital assistants (yes, I have seven such devices throughout my house) started defining "butterfly" for me. It rambled on about the insect and swimming stroke. The definition was quite thorough. The thing is, I didn't use the wake word, nor did I use the word "butterfly" in what I was saying.

My advice on the topic: If you're concerned about any of these things happening, even if the possibility is highly remote, don't bring one of these devices into your home. The simple matter is that any connected device, even created by the most well-meaning company on the planet for the most high-minded of purposes, can be compromised. This is advice at the extreme end of the spectrum, yet if you're worried about your private data getting into the wrong hands, it's best not to create that data in the first place.

Your IoT Security Checklist

However, with the upsides being what they are, you might want a home assistant, or a Wi-Fi enabled oven, or, yes, a smart coffee

---

[125] https://www.techworld.com/security/does-amazon-alexa-listen-to-my-conversations-3661967/

[126] Ibid.

[127] https://www.theverge.com/2018/12/20/18150531/amazon-alexa-voice-recordings-wrong-user-gdpr-privacy-ai

maker that can brew on demand from your phone. (Cue heavenly chorus!) And that's absolutely fine, but just be sure to protect those devices. Here's a list of things you should do:

- **Research devices before you purchase them.** Consider what data they may collect, how the manufacturer protects data, if they share it with anyone, and if they have a good track record of producing secure, privacy-centric devices. If you skipped ahead to this chapter, I encourage you to give chapter 5 a good read because it talks about these aspects of data collection and privacy in more exact terms, which still apply here.

- **Immediately change the user name and password on any IoT device you purchase.** Too many manufacturers ship their devices with a stock user name and password, which are known to the world thanks to the internet. A quick search can turn up plenty of examples of this stock user name and password combinations for a plethora of connected devices, which gives hackers a key into your network.[128] To give you an idea of just how fast this happens, McAfee's threat research team purchased an off-the-shelf DVR system from a local retailer. They took it into their lab, connected it to the internet, and then turned it on along with a stopwatch. Within 64 seconds the device was crawled and compromised.

- **Also immediately update the firmware on the device you purchased.** Just like your computer and smartphone apps, these devices (hopefully) receive regular updates that include security fixes and improvements. Install these right away. Also be sure to apply these updates in the future as they become available.

- **Use security software that protects your devices.** I've offered this advice a few times elsewhere in this book, and it bears repeating here. A more comprehensive package will contain features that protect not only the computer you install it on but also other devices on the network. It will also include firewall protection, which monitors your home

---

[128] https://www.fastcompany.com/90164031/you-can-hack-almost-any-smart-device-with-a-google-search

network for suspicious traffic. Even if a device is infected, a firewall can prevent other devices on the same network from being attacked as well (like your computer or phone, for example).

- **Where you can, use two-factor authentication.** For example, many banks make one factor your user name and password and a second one is a text sent to your phone. Two-factor authentication or multi-factor authentication will provide an additional layer that you should always use wherever it's offered.

- **Whenever possible, use a home router that includes security for connected things or IoT devices for your entire home.** This affords protection to what are referred to as headless devices or devices that don't have the means to install security software.

Beyond what I've outlined here, you may wonder about why it's important to protect even the most innocuous of connected things on your home network, like light switches that you can turn on and off from your smartphone. One Las Vegas casino found out the answer to that question the hard way, when a smart thermometer in a casino aquarium led to the heist of data about high rollers:

> *Nicole Eagan, CEO of cybersecurity company Darktrace, revealed Thursday that a casino fell victim to hackers thanks to a smart thermometer it was using to monitor the water of an aquarium they had installed in the lobby[.] The hackers managed to find and steal information from the casino's high-roller database through the thermometer.*

> *"The attackers used that to get a foothold in the network," Eagan said at a Wall Street Journal panel. "They then found the high-roller database and then pulled that back across the network, out the thermostat, and up to the cloud."*

> *That database may have included information about some of the unnamed casino's biggest spenders along with other private details, and hackers got a hold of it thanks to the internet of things.[129]*

---

[129] https://mashable.com/2018/04/15/casino-smart-thermometer-hacked/#mMowCsPTBaqJ

In other words, more connected devices open up more points of attack, or what's often referred to as an expanding attack surface, that a hacker can level at your network because its only as strong as your weakest link. You probably don't have a high-roller database in your home network, but you do have all manner of personal information in there, along with family photos, finances, and the like. You'll want comprehensive coverage across all the devices on your network, even the most seemingly innocent.

Overall, the final point for you to consider about IoT devices is "What's the tradeoff?" You can see now that expanding the number of connected devices introduces different risks to varying degrees—it generates more personal data about you and your family and how you live your lives, it can literally open up eyes and ears into your home via a camera and microphone on a home assistant device, and it offers hackers more points of attack that they can use to target your network and what you have stored on it. While I don't encourage you *not* to use them, just consider what conveniences you *really* need in your home. That will help you keep the growing number of connected devices in check to an amount that you're comfortable with. Not everything *needs* to be connected. Folks of the "Greatest Generation" had to get up from their chair to change the channel and they did just fine. Likewise, you get to decide for yourself which digital conveniences do or don't work for you, your lifestyle, and the effort you need to put in to support and protect them.

Silver Surfers—Protecting the Seniors in Our Lives

Speaking of our parents and grandparents, let's take a look at their safety and privacy online too.

There comes an interesting point in life where roles can reverse—where the child becomes the parent to his or her mom or dad. And it can creep up on you. As our parents and grandparents get older, we may find that we're helping them with caring for their homes, their finances, their health, and simply with getting from here to there. Even if we have the most independent of parents, we're inclined to offer our support or find ourselves lending it when it comes to matters of technology.

We give them advice about what phones or computers to buy, how to set up their internet, what apps they should use, and what software they need to protect themselves. My answer to my mom for almost every question she asks is, "there's an app for that." In the way that our kids are often savvier than we are about the digital world, we're that much savvier than the older generations in our families, the so-called silver surfers. We've grown up in the connected world in ways they have not, and we simply see it differently and know how to steer them through it because we're active, moment-to-moment participants in it.

In the last chapter we discussed the "family CIO" who covers your network, your devices, how they're used, who's using them, their security, the privacy of your data—all of that. In a lot of cases, those family CIOs also have the added responsibility to provide advice and hands-on expertise to their elderly parents and siblings. I recall when Equifax announced that they had been breached and some 146 million records containing Social Security numbers, date of birth, address, and in some cases driver's license numbers were exposed.[130] A week after that announcement I was visiting my mom. I asked her if she had heard about the breach. She said she had and expressed how terrible it was. My follow-up question was, "What did you do in response to the news?" She answered, much to my chagrin, "Nothing." I stepped her through the process of going to the three credit bureau websites to freeze her credit and how she should monitor her bank and retirement accounts for suspicious transactions. If you're wondering if this was a one-time thing with us, it's not. We often have discussions spanning everything you can imagine from good password management hygiene to what the latest scams are that she should be looking out for.

Taking an active role in mom's, dad's, grandma's, or grandpa's digital life is important. Findings from Pew Research Center shows that internet usage by seniors has risen from an average of 14% in 2000 to 67% on average 2017. What's more, this newly minted set of internet users may find themselves hopping online without having the benefit of "The Talk" (see chapter 2) that we gave our own children about the internet and steps they can take to stay safe and

---

[130] https://en.wikipedia.org/wiki/Equifax

protect their privacy while using it. In other words, some of the seniors in your life could be going online without some basic information and knowledge of behaviors that can keep them safe.

Have "The Talk" with Seniors Too

Because many seniors are still learning their way around the internet just as our kids are, I suggest having "The Talk" with them too, at least in some form. It doesn't have to happen all at once. And you can bring it up in any number of natural ways, like when they ask about upgrading their phone or when you're troubleshooting a problem with their computer or router. It's another "teaching moment"—except you're doing the teaching and they're doing the learning, which is entirely OK, especially when it comes from a place of caring and isn't done in a preachy way.

Much of the same information we share with our kids about staying safe applies to seniors as well: use strong passwords (with the aid of a password manager app), keep an eye out for suspicious emails and don't click on bad links, use security software, act on notifications from vendors they might be using that have been breached, check privacy settings, and be careful of what they share online. Essentially, the overwhelming majority of what we've discussed so far in this book applies to them. They have just as much to lose if their information or identity gets compromised. In fact, most probably have a lot more to lose as they are typically on a fixed income and run the risk of being ruined financially if a cybercriminal is able to access their bank or retirement accounts.

I'll add a few more items just for silver surfers, though. Let's talk about scams.

Even before the days of the internet, seniors have found themselves as the mark in scams. (Although it's important to note that anyone can be a victim of a scam, so what's included here is valuable at every age.) They tend to be a bit more trusting (or at least trusting of people who they believe to be in authority), which makes it easier for scammers to impersonate tax collectors, credit card companies, or technicians at "Microsoft" who have identified an issue with their computer and who can fix it for the low cost of

$1,200. In the U.S., the FBI also cites other psychological and economic factors that make them an attractive target as well, such as scams that offer low-cost prescriptions or cures, plus the fact that some seniors may sit on savings and investments. According to the National Cyber Security Alliance and the Better Business Bureau,[131] some of the most prolific scams aimed at seniors fall into one of the follow categories:

- Tech support scams where a scammer will call and claim to represent a well-known tech company (like Microsoft) and make a high-pressure pitch about fixing a (nonexistent) problem that they've identified with the senior's computer. They can encourage the installation of malware, ask for remote access to their computer, or simply grift a credit card number (and payment!) from them. No reputable tech company will ever contact people with a cold call to offer technical support service.

- Tax scams that direct seniors to make a payment, whether online or with a physical check sent to a scammer's post office box. Just know that in the U.S., the IRS will never reach out to you over email, nor will they call and require payment.

- Ransomware scams where a senior clicks on a bad link, whether from a scammer email or simply by surfing onto the wrong site while searching online. This results in ransomware malware getting installed on their computer that encrypts key files, which the scammer will only decrypt once a ransom is paid. "Ransomware is a type of malicious software from cryptovirology that threatens to publish the victim's data or perpetually block access to it unless a ransom is paid."[132] The best way for seniors to avoid this is to have strong security software installed on their device, which can warn them of bad links and skim away phishing emails designed to lure seniors to disreputable sites. Also, they can benefit from some of the anti-phishing advice I shared toward the end of chapter 3.

---

[131] https://www.protectseniorsonline.com/resources/hottest-cyber-scams/
[132] https://en.wikipedia.org/wiki/Ransomware

- False debt collection notices also make their way to the inboxes of seniors. This is another "confidence" play, where the scammer assumes the identity of a legitimate organization or creditor and makes threats around a lapsed or missed payment of some stripe. Again, delete these emails right away. And if there's any concern as to whether or not there is a legitimate debt collection issue, you can simply call the organization or creditor directly.

- Sweepstakes and charity scams play on emotions as well, the strings of which fraudsters pull to get seniors to hand over their banking information or credit card number. A "sweepstakes" will ask for banking information so they can send a payment. A "charity" will also grift a credit card number from the senior. As with all the other scams, if the communication stinks of something fishy or cannot properly prove that there's a legitimate business behind it, ax the email or end the call.

- Holidays, major sporting events, and, sadly, even natural disasters, tend to rally scammers and cyber crooks looking to take advantage of all the noise. Consider this irony: a holiday like Valentine's Day that is intended to engender love and happiness instead generates a spike in illicit activities. Niraj Chokshi with the *New York Times* states, "Americans looking for love lost at least $143 million to scammers last year, according to reports filed with the Federal Trade Commission. While those reports accounted for only 1.5 percent of all fraud tracked by the agency, no other type of scam wreaked as much financial havoc as those rooted in romance."[133] Most of the scams use a technique known as catfishing, where the perpetrator lures an unsuspecting individual into a relationship using a fake online persona. "People ages 40 to 69 reported losing money to romance scams at the highest rates, but those 70 and older were hardest hit, suffering a median loss of $10,000. Scam victims from the ages of 20 to 29 reported a median loss of about $1,000, the agency said."[134]

---

[133] https://www.nytimes.com/2019/02/13/business/ftc-online-romance-scams.html
[134] Ibid.

There's one other scam on the rise that has ties to social media use and privacy, not just of seniors, but of their family members as well. According to the U.S. Federal Trade Commission (FTC), roughly $41 million was lost to criminals who did their research using social media and other publicly available information to create a detailed profile of the victim and one of his or her family members, commonly a grandchild. The criminals then pose as an authority figure (a police officer, an attorney, or a doctor) and state that a member of the senior's family is "in trouble." From a CBS News report, one such story unfolded as follows:

"I'm the last person, I thought, would ever fall for a scam like this," Franc Stratton told CBS News correspondent Anna Werner.

The retired Tennessean spent his career working in intelligence, first for the Air Force and later as a cybersecurity programmer. But his expertise still didn't prepare him for the scam that began with a morning phone call in April.

"I hear, 'Don't be afraid, but I'm the public defender from Austin, Texas. They have put your grandson in jail after a wreck, and he has a DUI offense,'" Stratton said.

The man said Stratton could bail out his grandson if he sent $8,500 cash via FedEx, something that might sound ridiculous, except that Stratton had actually done just that for a family member once in the past.

Not only that, but the "attorney" briefly put his "grandson" — who sounded injured — on the phone. So, Stratton drove to the bank.

"I wrote a check out, and they gave me $8,500 cash in hundreds," Stratton said.

Then he went to a local mail location to overnight the money to an Austin address. Stratton said he fell for it "because of the way that they scripted it."

"They had it so well scripted. They knew everything about my grandson. They knew everything about me," Stratton said.[135]

---

[135] https://www.cbsnews.com/news/impostor-scam-targeting-grandparents-mailing-cash/

Some of the best advice to give our folks and grandparents is advice they likely know quite well already—be skeptical. Add to that by showing them some examples of just how sophisticated these attacks are and how *good* they can look, even though they aren't. (Head over to Phishing.org for some examples.[136]) I think healthy skepticism is key. We don't want them to feel like the digital world is "out to get them." Yes, they should be cautious and aware, but the internet is not a "bad" place. Absolutely, there are scams, scammers, identity thieves, fraudsters, etc. out there on the internet, but we needn't live in fear of them. Instead, we can simply apply what we have learned and go about our business with care.

The Mother of All Fraud: Social Security Scams

Social Security scams warrant an entire section due to the overwhelming impact they can have when successful. Social Security is a major source of income for the elderly in the United States. According to the Social Security Administration (SSA), "Nearly nine out of ten individuals age 65 and older receive Social Security benefits."[137] Most retirees are on a fixed income and any disruption in that income could have dire consequences.

Kiplinger suggests why scammers and cybercriminals target Social Security, "The Social Security Administration is a treasure trove for hackers. The agency holds data on nearly every American, averages about 70 million monthly beneficiaries, and paid roughly $1 trillion in benefits in fiscal 2018, mostly through electronic transactions. And like many organizations across the public and private sector, the agency is pushing customers to use its online services even as it struggles to stay a step ahead of cyber crooks."[138]

One would hope that bad actors would not target those reliant on Social Security to make ends meet, but that's not the case. According to Kiplinger, fraudsters are getting even more brazen with Social Security scams:

---

[136] http://www.phishing.org/phishing-examples
[137] https://www.ssa.gov/news/press/factsheets/basicfact-alt.pdf
[138] https://www.kiplinger.com/article/retirement/T051-C000-S004-social-security-scams-growing-threat-to-retirement.html

As the Social Security Administration strives to serve more customers online, the agency and current and future Social Security beneficiaries face the growing threat of cyber-attacks. Social Security identified nearly 63,000 likely fraudulent online benefit applications in fiscal 2018, according to the agency's Office of the Inspector General, up from just 89 in fiscal 2015. From February 2013 to February 2016 (the most recent data available), the Inspector General received more than 58,000 fraud allegations related to My Social Security accounts—an issue that persists today, according to the OIG. Meanwhile, there has been exponential growth in Social Security imposter scams, in which fraudsters claiming to be Social Security staffers contact victims—often via robocalls—and try to extract money or personal details. More than 35,000 people reported such scams in 2018, according to the Federal Trade Commission, up from 3,200 a year earlier."[139]

Making matters worse, the latest tactic of scammers attempts to paint you as a criminal—and *USA Today* reports it's using a U.S.-Mexico border angle:

Consumers are getting alarming phone calls from someone who claims to be from law enforcement or Social Security and then scares you into thinking that your Social Security number has been connected to running drugs and money laundering across the border.

The scam tries to convince you that your Social Security number has been suspended because of suspicious activity or because it's connected to a serious crime.

In some cases, your caller ID may show the real SSA phone number — 800-772-1213 — when the scammers call. But again, the con artists are able to spoof this number and make it look more legitimate.[140]

If you haven't already done so, I encourage you to create an account with the Social Security Administration[141] or sign in if you already have one and turn on two-factor authentication. Routinely log in and look for any suspicious activities. Also, whenever you get a call from someone saying they are with law enforcement or the

---

[139] Ibid.

[140] https://www.usatoday.com/story/money/2019/02/08/social-security-scam-calls-2019-latest-scheme-makes-you-criminal/2803136002/

[141] https://secure.ssa.gov/RIL/SiView.action

SSA, do not divulge any personal information. Instead, if you believe it may be something legitimate, go online to the appropriate website and locate the "contact us" page. From there you can call them directly or choose other ways to communicate with them. Large government agencies like the IRS and SSA tend to rely heavily on the U.S. postal service to provide notices to consumers. Be very wary when it looks like they're starting to call or email you directly.

What Did We Learn?

Thousands of once "dumb" devices now connect to the internet and have gotten "smart" in the process. With appliances, door locks, and light switches all available in internet-connected form, you can take care of numerous tasks right from your smartphone, home assistant, or both. Yet many manufacturers haven't fully grasped the security and privacy considerations associated with internet connectivity, perhaps because they're new to the space. They know coffee makers and lamps, but they don't know hackers and security protocols or what security controls need to be in place with their connected device. Even when they do, they may skip implementing those security controls in order to get first to market with their new gadget or in an effort to beat competitors and capture the hearts of customers first. Not all of them are up to speed on security. Not just yet. In the meantime, that places the responsibility on you to secure those devices by taking the steps outlined in this chapter. In fact, back in 2014 HP conducted research looking at the top connected devices deployed in the home and found, on average, they had 25 vulnerabilities each.[142]

The other consideration is your privacy. Using these connected IoT devices generates data from which others can infer all manner of information about you, such as when you come and go from your home and aspects of your daily routine in general. Adding a home assistant into the mix opens up other privacy concerns due to voice activation features. In all, using IoT devices comes with a tradeoff of convenience at the cost of privacy. It's up to you to understand

---

[142] https://www.computerworld.com/article/2476543/cybercrime-hacking/researchers-find-about-25-security-vulnerabilities-per-internet-of-things-device.html

what exactly is getting collected, who's using it, what they're doing with it, if it's being shared, with whom, and how it's protected all along the way. (Echoes of chapter 5 there.) Make the informed choice.

Finally, we're finding that seniors, our silver surfers, may be going online without the benefit of some baseline knowledge about security and privacy online. As their children and grandchildren, we've spent years online learning its ins and outs, and thus we have the opportunity to teach them and guide them about internet usage, just as they have taught (and continue to teach) us plenty about life. It's no surprise then that hackers have their favorite scams they like to level at these folks. Alerting seniors to what they are and what they look like can help them steer clear of trouble and enjoy their life online.

8

DIGITAL AFTERLIFE

We've lost people in our lives and seen them live on.

Through their relationships, contributions, actions, and memories of what they brought to our time together, they leave a lasting legacy.

Maybe you've seen a few legacies live on in your digital world too. I certainly have, where a friend who has passed away still has a Facebook page maintained by a loved one, or where another old friend from high school has pictures left behind in a class reunion group. I've also seen groups of families and friends spin up memorials and gathering places online, typically around the anniversary of their loved one's passing, where people can share their stories and pictures. Even people who had never met face-to-face will honor the memory of a friend with a posting in a blog or online forum where they shared some time and conversation together. We all grieve. And we all like to remember. The internet provides us with another place to do both and take comfort in others.

Something else has happened with the advent of the internet. People now form strong friendships with others through online games or other means. Specifically with gamers, they have spent potentially hundreds of hours together exploring a sprawling game world populated by thousands of other players at once, peppered with text and voice chatting along the way. As I discussed in the chapter on tweens and teens, these relationships are quite real, despite the fact that one player may live in Kansas and another in Manitoba. Understandably, when we lose an online friend, we mourn him or her like any other, so we now see memorial services being held within the game worlds that players shared, which sometimes even extend to the grieving family, as reported in this article on the topic published by *The Independent*:

> *One of the most notable examples saw Final Fantasy XIV players gathering to pay their respects for 29-year-old player [with the in-game name of] Codex Vahlda …*
>
> *Standing side-by-side, the group of friends gathered at a beach in the game, spelled out the name "Codex" on the messaging system and put on a light show. This virtual mourning was then streamed into the player's hospital room for the family to see.[143]*

Can you imagine the warmth that family must have felt at that moment, knowing their loved one had touched dozens upon dozens of other lives that they, arguably, had no idea about? Cynics might snicker at the thought of such displays in an online game. I call them wrong. The grief and the willingness to commune together are absolutely genuine and real. They just express themselves differently online, in this case a game. I think it's wonderful—and a testament to one of the more positive and powerful aspects of the internet.

A number of times over the course of this book I've said something to the effect of, "What goes on the internet is forever." That was said in the spirit of privacy, such as being careful about what you share, because once it's posted on the internet it's up there for good. Clearly, there's another dimension to that as well, where we're reminded that there are other people, and other lives, on the other side of that screen.

---

[143] https://www.independent.co.uk/life-style/online-funerals-gamers-friends-never-met-gaming-death-social-network-world-of-warcraft-skyrim-a7507836.html

Let's talk about that notion in highly pragmatic terms—your data lake and all the information and accounts you've created throughout your life. What becomes of the things you've posted, the things you've shared, and the things you've accrued online? They certainly don't vanish. Not at all. Put simply, when you pass away, you leave your data lake behind.

Digital Estate Planning

Just as you plan for the transfer of physical and financial assets to your loved ones, you should also add your digital assets and accounts to that list. As you can imagine, this is a relatively new concept, yet today we find ourselves holding umpteen digital assets that may be relatively intangible yet are no less valuable. Our online accounts have squirrelled away their fair share of assets that require handling and disbursement. We have airline miles, balances in PayPal accounts, family photos archived in online cloud storage, valuable or sentimental files locked away on a password-protected computer, movies and music purchased and downloaded from online stores, even digital books, and much more. Take a quick second to think about it—we've accrued much in our digital lives too, which we'll want to pass along.

Here's one example: you have a fantastic collection of classic rock albums that you've digitized into MP3 format. Years ago, you pulled your CDs off the shelf and ripped each of them onto your computer. After that, you chucked the CDs into a couple of milk crates and popped them into storage. Now, in effect, you have two instances of every Thin Lizzy, Pink Floyd, Cream, and Doors album you have in your collection—one physical, one digital. Each collection is an asset. How will you divvy those up? (And remain mindful of copyright laws in the process?) Importantly, who will have the password to the computer they're stored on?

Here's another: say you've picked up a small yet devoted following by blogging. Over the years you've posted regularly, every week or so. When you pass away, how would you like to see that blog live on? Would you want an announcement made and for a family member to maintain that blog site so that others can enjoy it years later? Or would you simply want it taken down? Questions like these come up when we pause and think about our passing. As we look back on our legacy, we see that we've left our mark on the digital world as well.

Another important consideration in this mix is one of security and privacy. Although you may no longer be in the physical world, the digital world is still alive with activity, so you'll want to protect your heirs and others from identity theft, doxing (where digital documents belonging to a person are dumped on the internet *en masse*), scammers; reputational harm, and digital asset takeover (where someone hijacks one or more of your accounts). Getting your digital ducks in a row right now can help prevent all those possibilities.

I suggest that you think of this as part of your regular estate planning rather than as a supplement to it. Digital assets are assets just like any other, and the process for listing them and including them in a will is much the same. You'll want a trusted individual to execute on your behalf, and you'll want to provide them with the accounts, information, and legal agency to act. One way to get started is to write up a summary of all your online accounts, passwords, and what assets are associated with them. (If you're using password management software, you can simply include that information.)

This will give the trusted individual who has power of attorney or who is your executor an overview of, and access to, your accounts so that they can follow your wishes for how you'd like those accounts and assets handled. You can make the estate process easier to manage for all parties involved. A Place for Mom, the largest senior living referral service in the U.S. and Canada, provides excellent guidance for the information to include for a power of attorney or will:

1. List of all account numbers, banks and institutions that are managed online.
2. List of all credit card accounts managed online including the name of the card issuer and card number.
3. List of cloud photo storage software/website and password.

4. List of email, internet and messaging programs used and their passwords.
5. List of monthly subscriptions and their passwords, i.e. Amazon Prime, Netflix, etc.
6. List of social media accounts and passwords.
7. Master password for your password saver software or list of current passwords.
8. Passwords for audiobook software if separate from phone operating system or another online account such as Amazon.
9. Passwords for music software such as Amazon Music, iTunes or Spotify.
10. Phone unlock code and operating system password.
11. URLs of online journals or individual blog articles.[144]

I'll add a few more items of my own:

12. Map out how you would like your digital assets distributed and how you would like to see them used. For example, maybe you want an online friend of yours to take over your blog, and thus bequeath her your password and admin privileges. Likewise, call out who has access to your family photos on Shutterfly.
13. Be clear about what you want done with your social media accounts. You can close all of them down if you wish, or you can elect to keep one up as a sort of memorial with its privacy selected to friends and family only.
14. Also, be clear overall as you detail your wishes for your digital assets. If you don't list them out and state your plans for them, it can result in months of legal wrangling to clear up your affairs. It can also result in your heirs never receiving them at all.
15. If it makes sense, consider adding a digital executor to your estate. You may find that you have a great deal of digital assets that will require additional effort and technical expertise that could otherwise overwhelm your primary executor.

---

[144] https://www.aplaceformom.com/blog/protect-your-digital-assets-after-death/

16. Get professional guidance when constructing your estate plan, along with your last will and testament. This guidance can take the form of an attorney, of course, or your bank or financial advisor. And now there are online estate planning services like LegalZoom or Rocket Lawyer, which provide the legal forms you need, along with guidance and, in some cases, telephone consultations from a legal professional who partners with the service.

17. Review your plan regularly. We pick up and cast-off digital assets and accounts with regularity nowadays, with greater speed than many of our physical assets, so keep your affairs in order for your heirs by periodically updating your digital assets in your estate plan.

Yes, that's quite a list. However, many of these activities fall in parallel step with all of your other estate planning activities, so it's likely you'll see some helpful overlap between the two. You'll also find that planning your digital estate lends itself to good digital hygiene as well. Simply listing your assets and gathering together your passwords helps you keep better track of your digital life and may prompt you to close some dusty old accounts or revisit the privacy settings on the current ones you use most.

What Did We Learn?

You have a digital legacy. And like any other legacy, you need to factor that into your estate planning. With a data lake the size of yours at this stage in life, you'll want to list out your assets and accounts, detail your wishes for them, and set that all forth in your will. You may also want to assign a digital executor to work with the primary executor of your will—usually if you believe your digital estate is too large or too complicated for one executor to handle. In all, get to thinking a little differently about the digital things you own. Although they may not be something you can pick up and hold, they still maintain plenty of value.

CONCLUSION

So, there you go. What started as an innocent data puddle with data trickling in has become a massive data lake filled to the brim with a lifetime of your personal information. Do you like what you see, or would you prefer a much smaller lake that was more carefully managed? Are the coyotes that lurk on the fringes of your lake becoming increasingly invasive? My hope is that you will use this book as a guide to build the behaviors and muscle memory needed for making your data lake right for you and your loved ones and keeping the coyotes at bay. Further, I hope that you will share the insights you take away from this book and use them to help members of your family and your community live more safely online.

The one thing I have learned over my years of being a security practitioner is that the biggest gap we have in realizing a more secure and privacy-empowered internet is a population of educated and informed users. If we can get society as a whole to think about and behave in ways that make it extremely difficult to be a victim, entire hosts of cybercriminals and scammers across the world will have to find real jobs. Only then will we be able to reap the true value and benefits of the always-on internet and everything we connect to it.

I'm reminded of a time when some colleagues of mine helped law enforcement take down a cybercriminal botnet (a network of private computers and devices infected with malicious software unbeknownst to their owners' knowledge). As we worked to pull data from the servers that the crooks kept, we found information on one of their victims. We went to the victim's home with local law enforcement and presented him with what we had found, which was literally everything imaginable about this individual—all his usernames and passwords, address, answers to security questions, date of birth, mother's maiden name. You name it, we had it. The question he asked was both profound and prosaic, "What do I do?" Therein lies the true nature of the importance of managing your digital lake with an eye toward keeping your data secure and information private. The last thing you want is to wake up one day to be presented with the stark reality that everything about you is a keystroke away from tearing your life apart.

With a wince, I say that man was lucky. You see, cybercrime is a borderless crime. The perpetrators may be based in one region of the world, host their technologies across a multitude of other geographic locations, and target victims in yet another. When people first hear this, they often pause and take a moment to grasp that notion. We still think of crime as being something rather local, but the scope of cybercrime is international, and proximity no longer matters. Moreover, it's big business. Really big business.

Large-scale criminal organizations have cropped up to cash in on the opportunities they see on the internet, backed by complex operations that mirror the operations of legitimate businesses. For example, a ransomware ring can have their own developers to create the malware, marketers to lure people in, and even "customer service" personnel who engage with the victims. For these reasons, businesses and law enforcement face an almost vertical uphill climb because many elements of the crime are committed across borders and are thus beyond the reach of their jurisdiction. Evidence eludes legal search and seizure, and perpetrators go about their "business" with little fear of prosecution. Thus, our botnet victim was "lucky" in that, in this case, we were able to seize the data and make him aware of what was stolen from him.

I bring this up because there's a popular image of the hacker—a young kid in a hoodie, hunched over a laptop in a dark and shoddy apartment. It's an image we see often, yet it's only partly accurate. There are indeed such lone wolves (or coyotes as we reflected earlier) committing cybercrime, but the most significant threat comes in the form of those large-scale organizations I mentioned above. As the digital world has grown, major crime has moved in and the age-old offenses of fraud, extortion, and theft have taken modern form. In fact, the economic impact of cybercrime in 2017 was $600 billion or .8% of the global domestic product.[145] Think of all the jobs and other opportunities that are displaced so companies are able to build stronger defenses against cybercriminal organizations and nation-state actors. Put plainly, major crime has adapted to the times just as it always does. And money isn't the only thing those criminals are after. In 2015 in the UK, cybercrime accounted for 53% of all criminal activities where "low-level crooks rely on 'the growing online criminal marketplace, which provides easy access to sophisticated and bespoke tools and expertise, allowing these less skilled cybercriminals to exploit a wide range of vulnerabilities.'"[146] Today, data and identity are currency too—just as we have illustrated throughout this book.

NBC recently reinforced the notion that data and identity are a new currency by reporting, "As we've seen in the past few years, data can predict not just which shirt you might be willing to buy, but which topics are so emotionally charged you cannot look away from them — and which pieces of propaganda will work best upon you. And that makes the platforms that collect data at scale an amazing way to influence human beings. Maybe not you. Maybe not today. But it's enough influence, at scale, over time, that the outcomes on the whole are both overwhelmingly consistent, and yet individually invisible."[147]

You can take comfort in knowing that cybersecurity companies and businesses have adapted as well. They're banding together and sharing anti-crime and threat intelligence among themselves and with law enforcement agencies across the globe. Large enterprises protect their customers and combat cybercrime by using layered

[145] https://www.csis.org/analysis/economic-impact-cybercrime
[146] https://www.fedscoop.com/brits-say-cybercrime-outstripping-its-offline/
[147] https://www.nbcnews.com/business/business-news/why-data-not-privacy-real-danger-n966621

security measures and dedicated business units that apply a combination of civil actions and criminal referrals to law enforcement in an effort to make the internet a safer place. Likewise, legislators have made efforts to update and create digital laws, plus get extradition agreements in place with other nations such that they can reach across borders when it comes time to prosecute.

Thus, if we think back to the introduction of this book and our analogy that the internet is like any neighborhood (with places to gather, places to play, places to shop, along with a few back alleys that we ought to avoid), it's encouraging to know that the upstanding members of the community have rallied around the cause of a safer internet. There's plenty more work that needs to get done on everyone's part—businesses, governments, law enforcement, and you—for the internet to grow into an even safer, more private neighborhood that we can all call home. Indeed, some of that work rests with us as individuals who step up and make our own effort to make ourselves and our families safer. Without question, a better, safer internet is a collective responsibility.

The Silver Bullet for Security and Privacy

The question I get most often in my travels: "Is there such a thing as a security silver bullet or one thing that you can do to stay safe?" My answer has always been "No." However, as I reflect back on the chapters of this book, I would now say, "Yes. The one thing you can do to ensure the likelihood of a safe digital life is to embrace a security and privacy mindset." I'm reminded of *Mindset – The New Psychology of Success,* a great book by Carol S. Dweck, PhD, where she discusses the difference between a fixed mindset and growth mindset:

In a fixed mindset, students believe their basic abilities, their intelligence, their talents, are just fixed traits. They have a certain amount and that's that, and then their goal becomes to look smart all the time and never look dumb. In a growth mindset, students understand that their talents and abilities can be developed through effort, good teaching and persistence. They don't necessarily

169

think everyone's the same or anyone can be Einstein, but they believe everyone can get smarter if they work at it.[148]

I believe a security and privacy mindset closely follows the traits of a growth mindset in that to be successful in safeguarding your digital journey and managing your data lake, you need to always be thinking about what's next, staying informed, and educating yourself. A good question to ask yourself periodically: "How is the security and privacy space evolving and changing, and what steps should I take to keep me and my family safe in this changing world?"

A great example of how the security and privacy space is evolving is that the two disciplines are converging as technologies around big data and machine learning are being activated and becoming increasingly pervasive. You may have seen the television commercials where major industry players tout the benefits of artificial intelligence (AI), including how they use this machine learning to assist archaeologists on dig sites, help cities improve their traffic flow, and help coaches piece together a winning basketball team. There's truth in that. Yet there are privacy implications to AI as well. Andrew Burt, writing for *Harvard Business Review*, did a great job of framing up how the convergence of big data and AI affects our privacy:

More specifically, the threat of unauthorized access to our data used to pose the biggest danger to our digital selves — that was a world in which we worried about intruders attempting to get at data we wanted private. And it was a world in which privacy and security were largely separate functions, where privacy took a backseat to the more tangible concerns over security. Today, however, the biggest risk to our privacy and our security has become the threat of unintended inferences, due to the power of increasingly widespread machine learning techniques. Once we generate data, anyone who possesses enough of it can be a threat, posing new dangers to both our privacy and our security.

These inferences may, for example, threaten our anonymity — like when a group of researchers used machine learning techniques to identify authorship of

---

[148] https://jamesclear.com/fixed-mindset-vs-growth-mindset

written text based simply on patterns in language. (Similar techniques have been used to identify software developers based simply on the code they've written.)[149]

Burt goes on to say, "Once described by Supreme Court Justice Louis Brandeis as 'the right to be let alone,' **privacy is now best described as the ability to control data we cannot stop generating, giving rise to inferences we can't predict.**"[150] (Emphasis is mine.) Let me give you an example of what those inferences can look like in the real world and the impact they can have on people's lives. In this case a major U.S. retailer, Target, guessed that a daughter was pregnant before her father found out she was. As recounted by a statistician at Target in a *Forbes* article from 2013, the story goes like this when a father confronted the manager of a Target in the Minneapolis metro area:

"My daughter got this in the mail!" he said. "She's still in high school, and you're sending her coupons for baby clothes and cribs? Are you trying to encourage her to get pregnant?"

The manager didn't have any idea what the man was talking about. He looked at the mailer. Sure enough, it was addressed to the man's daughter and contained advertisements for maternity clothing, nursery furniture and pictures of smiling infants. The manager apologized and then called a few days later to apologize again.

(Nice customer service, Target.)

On the phone, though, the father was somewhat abashed. "I had a talk with my daughter," he said. "It turns out there's been some activities in my house I haven't been completely aware of. She's due in August. I owe you an apology."[151]

Now there's a reason that a statistician from Target is the one who shared this anecdote. As explained in the article, Target ties a

---

[149] https://hbr.org/2019/01/privacy-and-cybersecurity-are-converging-heres-why-that-matters-for-people-and-for-companies
[150] Ibid.
[151] https://www.forbes.com/sites/kashmirhill/2012/02/16/how-target-figured-out-a-teen-girl-was-pregnant-before-her-father-did/#5cfe95e76668

unique customer ID to shoppers, which it pairs with their credit card info, their address, and other personal information that Target has about that person—whether collected by Target or purchased from data brokers. Further tied to this ID is a shopping history. Taken together, along with millions of other IDs and shopping histories, Target can infer sometimes chillingly accurate information about shoppers based upon what passes over the checkout scanner. For example, Target knew that purchases of unscented body lotion, extra-big bags of cotton balls, and nutritional supplements like calcium, magnesium, and zinc often indicated that they were purchased for or by a woman whose delivery date is fast approaching. Note that all of this is legal. The question of whether it's *right* had the Target statistician echoing a cautionary note in the wake of this incident when he said, "We are very conservative about compliance with all privacy laws. But even if you're following the law, you can do things where people get queasy."[152]

Remember, this story hit the newsstands back in 2013. You've read this book, so you now know how the practice of data collection has exploded since then. (It's called big data today for a reason.) Add in the sophisticated advances in data analysis and AI and you can only wonder what businesses know, or can at least strongly infer, about you because you have a customer ID or a discount club card. This convergence of massive data capture and AI is happening now and having a security and privacy mindset will help you prepare for what that convergence will bring. But honestly, I'm not going to sugarcoat any of what I say here. It will take work. You will need to carve time out of your regular routine to learn and practice good digital hygiene. I can assure you, however, that you will be glad you did.

Your Security and Privacy Checklist

I'm a big fan of checklists. Always have been. I believe they serve to sustain rigor in what otherwise are considered mundane tasks and ensure a consistent application of discipline in key facets of our jobs and lives. If you think about it, some of our most sophisticated and complicated tasks, such as preparing to fly an airplane or perform a

---

[152] Ibid.

surgery, rely on a checklist to ensure everything is properly set and ready to go. In one of his best-selling books, *The Checklist Manifesto: How to Get Things Right,* Atul Gawande reflects: "Whether running to the store to buy ingredients for a cake, preparing an airplane for takeoff, or evaluating a sick person in the hospital, if you miss just one key thing, you might as well not have made the effort at all."[153]

My personal security and privacy checklist for every day includes the following tasks:

1. Scan the news for breaking security and privacy reports that suggest I need to take an action.
2. Apply any system or application updates to my devices.
3. Scan my bank and investment accounts for any suspicious transactions.
4. Check my identity monitoring service for any anomalies.
5. Launch my password manager so I can easily log into any accounts that I need access to during the day. My password manager also compares my passwords against known breached credentials so I can make any required changes.

Obviously, there are several other tasks I do regularly but not daily to safeguard my privacy and digital life. For example, I regularly go to the Have I Been Pwned (HIBP) website[154] and check to see if any of my accounts have been compromised in a data breach. The site currently lists roughly 6.5 billion accounts that have been indexed to help you determine if your accounts have been compromised. When I find an account on HIBP, I use my password manager to change the password unless it's associated with an account I no longer use, in which case I take steps to remove the account. Another feature of HIBP is their password checker, which connects you to a database of more than *half a billion* known passwords. Simply type in the password you wish to check and HIBP will tell you if it has shown up in a data breach at some point (and how many times). I hope it goes without saying that if you find the password being used that you will opt to use something different.

[153] http://atulgawande.com/book/the-checklist-manifesto/
[154] https://haveibeenpwned.com/

I encourage you to take some time to think through where you are in your digital journey and determine what's important to you, and then create your own security and privacy checklist. You may have young children or teens or perhaps elderly parents in need of your help and guidance, each of which would affect what you do on a daily or regular basis. Between your newly minted and engaged mindset and taking the time each day to work your checklist, you'll be well on your way to enjoying life online free of fear or anxiety of what lurks behind that next click.

In line with what has been reflected throughout this book: as your digital life evolves, you should regularly rethink your security and privacy checklist to have it reflect those tasks that are most important to you at any given point in your digital journey. It's important to not make an overwhelming checklist—the more complicated it is the less likely you will be to stick to it and to have it deliver the desired outcome.

What's Next

As I work toward wrapping this book up, I realize that the space this book is intended to help clarify and illuminate is changing. Virtually every day we learn about something new or different that reshapes the cybersecurity and privacy landscape. Literally as the ink dries, Facebook is in the process of combining the three messaging platforms they own (Messenger, WhatsApp, and Instagram) into one app. My mind is spinning with the privacy implications from this. I also see the latest craze in the video sharing app TikTok. Simply put, TikTok is a free, short-form video app popular with teens (or Generation Z, as they are known).[155] The app has skyrocketed with 1 billion downloads and over 500 million active users. I wonder how they will ensure their users are secure and their personal information is kept private as they continue to grow, especially when knowing the company that developed TikTok is in China, a country that historically has not put much emphasis on personal privacy.

---

[155]

https://www.theguardian.com/technology/shortcuts/2019/mar/11/tiktok-video-app-internet-500-million-users-social-media

We are also reminded, in a sobering *Washington Monthly* article by Judy Estrin and Sam Gill, that the world is on the brink of choking on all the digital pollution that is being created:

For all the good the internet has produced, we are now grappling with effects of digital pollution that have become so potentially large that they implicate our collective well-being. We have moved beyond the point at which our anxieties about online services stem from individuals seeking to do harm—committing crimes, stashing child pornography, recruiting terrorists. We are now face-to-face with a system that is embedded in every structure of our lives and institutions, and that is itself shaping our society in ways that deeply impact our basic values.[156]

Suffice it to say that issues will continue to arise as the internet grows and expands in ways that we can and cannot project. One thing that will remain a constant is our intrinsic desire to connect and share. It's human nature, and the very nature that birthed the internet in the first place. What I hope is that we find ourselves not only more able but more willing to exercise some control over what we share, when and where we share it, and with whom—all in an above-the-board and conscientious way.

Yup, that's some pie in the sky talk, yet if we at least align our actions and habits with that thinking, I'm certain that the internet will be far better off for it than if our current state of online affairs remains in place. If it was a combination of idealism, ingenuity, and plain-old hard work that gave the internet its rise, the same combination can give the internet its future. And because we all use the internet, we each have a responsibility to look after it by way of looking after ourselves and our loved ones who use it.

Looking ahead, I can see the need for a revision to this book soon, if not the need to write another one entirely as things change continually. I also see the need to build a gathering place online where we can regularly share out important information you can use to stay safe. More to come on that. Until then, thank you for doing your part to safeguard your digital journey and protect what matters

---

[156] https://washingtonmonthly.com/magazine/january-february-march-2019/the-world-is-choking-on-digital-pollution/

to you and your family. I genuinely hope you take the insights herein and make a better world for yourself and your loved ones. I also hope that you pay it forward by embracing what you've learned to create a culture of security and privacy so that your community and workplace will reap the benefits.

ABOUT THE AUTHOR

Gary Davis is Chief Consumer Security Evangelist at McAfee. He partners with internal teams to align McAfee's product development with the needs of consumers which drive meaningful advances in the security that improve people's lives. Gary also provides security education and awareness to businesses and consumers by distilling complex security and privacy topics into actionable advice.

He is a sought-after speaker on topics and trends in digital security including privacy, the evolving threat landscape, securing the internet of things, the challenges with cryptocurrency, and many more. He has presented at high-profile conferences and events, including CES, Mobile World Congress, SXSW, Silicon Slopes, and the National Association of Broadcasters. He has also delivered digital security topics to major educational institutions including Harvard University and Columbia University.

Gary has appeared on multiple business, security and consumer lifestyle broadcast outlets, including CBS News, CNBC, NBC, ABC, FOX News, ESPN, Bloomberg and WSJ MoneyBeat. He's also been quoted on CNN and in the *New York Times*, the *Wall Street Journal*, *USA Today*, *Money* magazine, *Forbes*, *Entrepreneur*, *U.S. News and World Report*, and *Time* magazine to name a few. He has also been featured on radio programs in markets across the country.

During his 10-plus years at McAfee, Gary has held leadership roles in the consumer and enterprise divisions, where he has helped shape various product portfolios and strategic direction along with advocating for cybersecurity and privacy education.

Prior to joining McAfee, he held senior management positions for 20-plus years in technology companies. Gary served on the board of directors of the National Cyber Security Alliance (NCSA).

76382261R00112

Made in the USA
Columbia, SC
24 September 2019